Are you girls TRAVELING ALONE?

Adventures in Lesbianic Logic

Marilyn Murphy

with an introduction by Marilyn Frye

Clothespin Fever Press

Los Angeles 1991

All of the selected essays appeared in various issues of the *Lesbian News*, see appendix for dates. Three, however, also appeared in the following publications:

"And Baby Makes Two" from *Politics of the Heart: a Lesbian Parenting Anthology*, edited by Sandra Pollack and Jeanne Vaughn (Firebrand Books, Ithaca, NY: 1987); "Mother of the Groom" also from *Politics of the Heart: a Lesbian Parenting Anthology*; "Looking for Lesbians" from *Finding the Lesbians* edited by Julia Penelope and Sarah Valentine (The Crossing Press, Freedom, CA 1990)

Clothespin Fever Press
5529 N. Figueroa, Los Angeles, CA 90042

First Edition

Cataloging information:

Murphy, Marilyn.

Are you girls traveling alone?
adventures in lesbianic logic

1. Lesbianism 2. Women's studies
306.7763

ISBN:1-878533-03-7

This book is dedicated to the women in my life.

My mother, Sally Murphy
My sisters, Jeanne, Sally Ann, Carol and Sharon
My daughters, Annie, Jeanne and Susan
My granddaughters, Kachina and Tahkus
My nieces, Caroline, Marilyn, Cynthia, Isla
My sisters-in-love, Sandra and Jacqui
My daughter-in-law, Jan
Sister Rose Edmond and Sister William Agnes,
St. Patrick's school, Long Island City, NY
The Dominican Sisters, St. Agnes Academy, College Point, NY
The friends of my non-Lesbian years
whose love helped me survive
Lesbian publishers, editors and writers
Jinx Beers
who asked me to write for the Lesbian News
Lynne Harper
Sagaris, Califia Community and Pagoda women
Lesbian friends who, like my biological family,
argue with almost everything I say, who teach, inspire,
encourage and entertain me, and who forgive me when I use
their lives in my writing

and Irene Weiss
my beloved companion
my sweet distraction
my severest critic
whose life and thoughts infuse everything I write.

TABLE OF CONTENTS

TABLE OF CONTENTS

PREFACE

Marilyn Murphy and I are only about a year apart in age. Thus we grew up in America during the same years, but on very different paths. Marilyn chose the more conventional road of marriage and motherhood -- after all, isn't that what women are taught as they are growing up in America? -- and enjoyed all the privileges of heterosexuality. Only of late, in her early forties, did she realize there were other options and became a Lesbian. A convert, as they say! I, on the other hand, learned very early (before age seven) that I was attracted to girls and never for a moment considered marriage or children. I'm a lifelong Lesbian who has always known who I was, or more accurately, what I wasn't, and have "enjoyed" all the discrimination of homosexuality.

Isn't it strange, then, that as Marilyn and I approach our sixtieth year of life, our philosophies have turned out to be very, very similar indeed. That's not to say that I agree with everything she says or writes, but I would and have defended her right to say it.

In 1982 Marilyn Murphy joined the staff of the growing, 7-year-old newsletter/magazine/newspaper **The Lesbian News** as a columnist. She was the only columnist to whom I ever gave space who had the freedom to write about anything she wanted, rather than a specific subject. And she was an instant hit -- or miss depending upon which side of the "Marilyn Murphy controversy" you happened to be on.

No other columnist before or since Marilyn has generated as many letters, as many comments, or has had as much time taken by the Editorial Board! Why? Because Marilyn has dared to give her opinion on topics no one else was ready to think about. She stirs the pot!

When I founded **The Lesbian News**, it was with a conviction that it was going to be a community news medium that was open to all opinions and to everyone who had something to say to the Lesbian/Feminist community. No censorship, very little editing, was the rule of the day. I looked upon **The Lesbian News** as a clearinghouse for ideas, events, happenings, and opinions of the Southern California community.

And in my nearly-fifteen years of stewardship, I believe I upheld that vision of the LN despite, or maybe because of, Marilyn's wonderful ability to articulate her personal opinion. I found over the seven or so years that Marilyn wrote for the LN under my editorship that no one was neutral about her. I had letters that threatened to stop reading the paper if we continued to give her space. I had letters that threatened to stop reading the paper if we ever discontinued her column. I had women who said they never read Marilyn's column, and those who declared Lesbianic Logic was the first item they turned to when each new LN hit the streets. Hey, ya gotta be doin' something right to generate this much notice!

What Marilyn does that is "right" is to open up topics for discussion. Some of her detractors say this is "divisive" in the community. I believe as Marilyn does, that a healthy community has the ability and obligation to discuss their differences. Intelligent and thoughtful communication heals the wounds that narrow-mindedness and self-aggrandizement in our community open. Marilyn doesn't spit out ideas for the sake of controversy; she researches and experiences and intelligently and thoughtfully shares her opinions so that others can join in the discussion and learn.

Except for a few libraries and personal collections, Marilyn's unique Lesbianic Logic has not been available for newcomers to read, or us old-comers to re-read, until now. The publication of this book opens a new and wonderful opportunity for us to look at ourselves and celebrate our differences as well as our community.

Jinx Beers
founder of **The Lesbian News**
Los Angeles, March 1991

INTRODUCTION

Two things that a great many women's studies students and community lesbians/feminists (not mutually exclusive classes) roundly dislike are "political correctness" and inaccessible academic feminist and lesbian theory. But paradoxically enough, sometimes the same woman who is pissed off and offended by anybody else's "politically correcting" her will turn right around and be pissed off and offended by academic feminist theory precisely because it is *politically incorrect*. She may not use exactly this phrase, but her complaint is that such theory does not empower, it may even disempower, her or other women in her situation. What she sees is that producing such theory is politically (pertaining to empowerment and liberation) incorrect (ineffectual, counter-productive or damaging).

This confusion of attitudes about political correctness is encouraged by several things, all having to do with the distance there usually is between carefully thought-out theory and the judgments and assessments we make in our ordinary personal and political interactions with each other.

Marilyn Murphy closes that gap. This collection of her articles is a sustained expression of commitment, serious but not humorless, to practical political correctness in all aspects of life and thought, and she is equally committed to clearly

11

and practically spelling out the perceptions, analysis, and political intuitions that ground her judgments and recommendations. By my lights, the politics that suffuses and unifies this work could be identified as a species of radical feminism, but I need to explain what I mean by that.

Though I am an academic and was a feminist by 1969, I managed to live for years without the knowledge that when academic feminists (and many participants in what was then called "Women's Liberation") used the term "radical feminism," they meant only to refer to a quite particular set of claims that were made--most uncompromisingly perhaps--by Shulamith Firestone in *The Dialectic of Sex* and Ti-Grace Atkinson in *Amazon Odyssey*. These claims were: that men's domination of women is the original and most fundamental social division and hierarchy; that all other dominance-subordinance divisions evolved from that and presuppose it; that the origin of men's domination of women is connected with the differences in female and male biological roles of reproduction; that the way to end all oppressions is to end the oppression of women by men, and that this can be done by socially, politically and technologically changing the practices and meanings of reproduction. These claims, articulated in books published in the early 1970s, have now been almost entirely rejected among feminists in the academy and most other feminists as well, and the term "radical feminist" is a term which almost no one in the academy would use to name or locate herself.

Oddly out-of-touch, I thought "radical feminist" meant "feminist to the root," "feminist all the way," "extremely feminist," or even "extremist feminist." I thought that if you took feminism absolutely seriously, embraced it wholly, and followed it courageously and logically (crone-logically or lesbianic logically) to its conclusions, you were a Radical Feminist.

Marilyn Murphy is my kind of Radical Feminist. Her understanding of the world bears some resemblance to what academics and early activists labelled "radical feminism"--she certainly thinks men's oppression of women is "fundamental" in many ways to many aspects of women's lives. She believes that men's oppression of women is very involved both as cause and as effect in the compulsory practices and dominant mores and meanings that govern reproduction and sex, and that alterations in these practices, mores, and meanings are a significant part of a viable strategy of liberation. But what makes her "very" feminist, or "extremist" feminist, hence radical in my own favored meaning of the word, is that her analysis evolves coherently from a central and passionate philogyny (the contrary of misogyny), an intelligent and engaged loving perception of women. And she proceeds courageously--to the extremes--to enact the values which her analysis supports.

This union and integration of analysis and action, this *lived theory*, does not separate politics from living. Every moment of living has meanings connected with our oppression, our resistance, our liberation. Where we live, how we get money, how we spend our money, who our friends are, what we eat, what we wear, what we do for fun, how we quarrel and how we make up, the art we make, who our lovers are and what we do with them, what organizations we participate in, how we relate to institutions of government and law, what rites and rituals we participate in, what we celebrate and how, and the language we use . . . always, everywhere, on any topic, the language and the languages we use . . . all of these things align our energies and powers with or against (or ambiguously with and against) oppression, resistance, liberation. When feminist theory is anything worth doing and worth listening to, it illuminates these alignments in ways that help us to locate ourselves deliberately and willfully, through everything we do, in opposition to our oppression and in support of our liberation. Radical feminists, I mean extremist feminists, want to produce such theory, for they want all of their personal resources--bodily energy, ardor, intelligence, understanding, vitality--to be available and engaged in the creation of a world for women. They want none of it to be turned back against women by the sometimes insidious, sometimes blatant, manipulations which systematically lock women into the service of men.

Radical feminist theorizing is endless because Everything Matters and Everything Is Connected. It carries you out to global economics and follows you into your bedroom, and it never stops. Every time you begin to feel good about getting something figured out and making the necessary changes, something else comes up. You might finally comprehend that the religious values you learned growing up were profoundly patriarchal and then begin learning about the spiritual practices and traditions of other cultures which are less patriarchal--or so you believe--only to find that you have unwittingly started participating in a trend of cultural colonization and exploitation of those cultures. You begin to learn to love and care for your body only to figure out that what you've started doing to "care for your body" (e.g., dieting) is in fact both physically destructive and traps you into self-loathing. These are what political correctness is about. If you aren't in this business radically, wholeheartedly, and for the long haul, political correctness can be mighty irritating.

Discerning what action, attitude, and stance are really liberatory, for ourselves and others, is almost never easy. We have been confused and misinformed, have been taught since the cradle values which promote our subordination rather than our liberation. To a large extent these learned values have even caught us up in the oppression of others. Because of this, we have to think and analyze and talk with each other endlessly about how to understand the information we have, how to assess our feelings and desires, how to change ourselves; we have to think together and discuss among ourselves what sorts of collective strategies are sound, are "cost-effective," are least prone to cooptation, and so on.

Everything is in question. Everything has to be created anew.

It is this talking, discussing, analyzing, assessing, re-describing, re-defining, judging, figuring out that I speak of that Marilyn Murphy is engaged in throughout all of her writing. Because the work is interminable, so challenging and so strenuous, you might expect it to be grim and bleak. Quite the opposite is true. Marilyn Murphy is spirited, witty, and passionate throughout, as are most of the radical Lesbian feminists she writes about. This work of critique and creation is energizing and healthful, the workers are strengthened and cheered by the work. As it turns out, a life of trying to be politically correct, at least as Marilyn Murphy has led it, is a life characterized by an unusual degree of freedom, the satisfactions of continual creativity, the rewards of stimulating companionship, and, we are allowed to suppose, good sex.

Marilyn Frye
Minneapolis, April 1991

I. Who We Are

COLOR ME LAVENDER *August, 1982*

[*This is the first article I wrote as a columnist for the* **Lesbian News** *in 1982. I thought it was important for readers to know some of the more significant facts about my life and beliefs which color my view of reality.*]

I was born, the first of five sisters, into a working class Italian/Irish Catholic family in New York City on June 19, 1932. For forty-three years, I lived a heterosexual life. I was a housewife and mothered three female and one male child to adulthood. I entered college at thirty-three years of age and quit nine years later with a rejected Ph.D dissertation on the lives and opinions of one hundred-fifty one California feminist activists. I am a radical feminist political activist, a Lesbian-Come-Lately living happily in a monogamous relationship with my companion lover who is a Lifelong Lesbian. From 1976 to 1986, I was a founding member of Califia Community, a radical feminist educational organization, and of the San Fernando Valley Rape Crisis Service as well. My two secret childhood ambitions were to sing in a nightclub in a sequined gown and to write an opinion column for a newspaper. I am very pleased to have the opportunity to realize one of them.

Because I am a Lesbian-Come-Lately, I sometimes think that Lifelong Lesbians do not "appreciate" Lesbianism, that they take Lesbian life for granted. This is their right, of course. They paid for it with the courage, ingenuity, determination and love it took to live a Lesbian life and develop a Lesbian network in the closet of pre-Women's Liberation Movement America. They paid for it again by the power and daring with which they forced open the Lesbian closet door within the Women's Liberation Movement. When I strolled down Lesbian Lane in 1975, the door to the Lesbian community was wide open; a "Welcome Home" sign hung in the window, and I could choose to live wherever and however I was comfortable. This is a privilege I pledge never to forget.

Still, some Lifelong Lesbians do sometimes take Lesbianism for granted. They tell me that, just because they prefer women as partners, it does not follow that they think women who relate to men cannot live as satisfying a life as Lesbians do. They state that some women are even more awful than some men are. Once in a great while, they say being a Lesbian is not worth the hassle. Some Lesbians beat their lovers, they argue, and some rape. Gender differences aside, they say, a relationship between two people is just that, a relationship. I respond with political theory and get THAT look from them, that "what do you know about it, newcomer," look.

To me, becoming a Lesbian is not a lateral move. Lesbian life and heterosexual life are not two houses on the same street, identical except for minor variations--one house has a fireplace, the other a skylight . No matter how similar they may appear on the surface, the differences between these two modes of being are profound. Every interaction between a woman and a man, from how to behave when a man holds the door open for you at the bank, to getting medical help for the husband who won't go to the doctor, has rules, guidelines, customs and traditions. Even non-traditional relationships between a woman and a man have rules, guidelines, customs and traditions, if only as something to rebel against. No matter what remodeling or extras, the house in which heterosexual life is lived was designed thousands of years ago to serve the needs of men, and will continue to serve men's needs until institutional male supremacy (patriarchy) is abolished.

Lesbian life, however, is lived in a totally different dimension. Everything is free-form for us. Our "out-of-the-law" status and our invisibility force us to create our own ways of relating vis-a-vis other Lesbians, even in the most mundane, everyday situations. There are no rules, guidelines, customs or traditions for women-loving women. The battering Lesbian, for example, cannot laugh with the "boys" when they joke, "Do you believe in clubs for women?" She cannot assuage her conscience with her knowledge of the Napoleonic law forbidding a husband to beat his wife with a stick wider than his thumb (the "rule of thumb"). She can't justify her behavior by thinking all women need a good trouncing once in a while. She has no assurance that the police, most of whom have wives, will identify with her and not jail her for punching out the "little woman." Even she must design her own Lesbian life.

I feel about Lesbianism as if I spent forty-three years being color blind, seeing the world in gradations of grey. At first I was intoxicated by the sight of the primary colors. I still am, but now I am able to see an ever-widening spectrum. I run around saying, "Look at all the varying shades of green. How brilliant! How subtle!" Some women, having seen color all their lives, are not impressed. "Big deal," they say. "I've seen some shades of green that were positively disgusting."

Or, to use a different simile, I am like a woman hearing music for the first time. I run around saying, "Hear that! Hear that! Now I can even recognize the flute sound accompanying the strings." And some women, having listened to music all their lives, are bored by my enthusiasm. "The first violin is flat," they say.

Of course these disclaimers do not stop me from remarking upon the colors and the music Lesbian life is to me. In my next life, when I am a Lifelong Lesbian, I may be blase about my good fortune too, though I do not really think so.

ARE YOU GIRLS TRAVELING ALONE?
April, 1984

"Are you girls traveling alone?" is the second most frequent question my companion lover and I are asked as we travel by RV around the country. "Where do you come from?" is number one. We are queried at our campsite, in campground bathrooms, on fishing piers and beaches, at gas stations and laundromats. We have heard it while enjoying the view from a variety of sightseeing vehicles: on a logging train on the way to see Tahquemenon Falls in Michigan; in the horse-drawn buggies of Charleston, South Carolina, St. Augustine, Florida, and Quebec; on the boats of Lake Superior, St. Lawrence River, Niagara Falls, the Bay of Fundy, the port of New Orleans. From Prince Edward Island Canada to the Florida Keys, when people see us and realize we are traveling in an RV, they seem impelled to ask us, "Are you girls traveling alone?

How can two middle-aged women possibly answer such a question? The implications in the question are inescapable. "Are you girls traveling alone?" Girls? Alone? We are together, obviously. We are obviously middle-aged.

When adults see children in places where children ordinarily do not go without their parents, we might say to them, "Are you girls here alone?" This is a "tactful" way of saying what we really mean: "What are you doing here, where you do not belong unless accompanied by adults who can protect you and keep you out of trouble and keep

21

you from bothering me?" I must admit to these feelings at times, especially when I find myself glancing over at where children, "alone," are playing in a potentially dangerous setting.

When we are asked the question, "Are you girls traveling alone?" the real question is an incredulous, "Are you traveling without men?" Although we are two women traveling together, we are perceived as one woman traveling without a man/husband and one other woman traveling without a man/husband. Our previous trips by car, train and plane have not elicited this question. Even six weeks in the British Isles raised no eyebrows that we could see. It seems to be an accepted practice there for women to "go someplace" together, and many of us do.

Certainly, in other settings, and at other times in my life since my early teens, the question, "Are you girls here alone?" asked by men, meant something different. Then, the implication was that to be there without a man -- that is, ALONE -- meant that we were looking for a man and were fair game for aggressive sexual advances for being there without male protectors.

The question asked by men in a camping setting or referring to our camping trip, however, has no sexual connotation. In fact, sexual innuendo has been remarkably absent from conversations with non-women in a camping environment. I think this is probably because activities associated with camping, fishing, hiking, hunting, boating, have little or no (hetero-) sexual content for men. Nonetheless, the masculine sensibility is deeply disturbed by our man-less presence, traveling with an RV, sightseeing, staying in remote campgrounds, doing TOGETHER whatever the men do, with or without "their" women. Their belief that their wives could not get along without them, especially while traveling in the family camper, motorhome, trailer, gets a terrific jolt when we are around.

The way men handle this situation is to assume that we cannot get along without them too. As soon as they realize we are "alone," they rush over to help us. Camping people have a reputation for helpfulness, but this is something else, something men do not do with other men. First, they give us advice about parking our vehicle -- we have had men actually offer to park our vehicle for us! (For non-campers: parking an RV can be tricky because the refrigerator must be level or it can be ruined, and ground has a tendency to be uneven.) They offer to light pilot lights, move picnic tables, carry wood, explain maps, give directions, make recommendations. They give us unsolicited advice on everything but cooking. So far, no man has offered to take out our garbage.

Most women who ask if we are traveling alone also mean are we traveling without men. Usually, women ask the real question, without the woman-erasure word, "alone." A couple of times, women tried to play incompetent child when they realized what we were doing. One, a woman in her fifties, tanned, thin and tough-looking, was so taken aback by our situation that she tried, unsuccessfully, to convince us that she was not "brave enough to travel around the country without my husband." Alas!

The more usual response from women to our man-less travel arrangements is first surprise and then delight -- especially if their husbands are not present. Many have been outright overjoyed. "What fun!" they say. "What a great idea," they say, and "How wonderful to travel without the men." They say, "No men? Now that's a great way to travel," and, "I wish I could travel with my girlfriend!" and "You girls sure know how to do it right." Two women at a produce stand in Nova Scotia were so thrilled by us that they loaded us down with their vegetables and charged us hardly anything. A woman in a supermarket in Monticello, New York, was so exuberant about our trip, so explicit about the advantages of traveling without men, that I actually began to feel sorry for her husband who was standing beside her, leaning on the shopping cart filled with purchases for their motor home parked in front.

While this response in front of a husband was unusual, the sentiments she expressed were not. Women are very frank about having more fun when they go someplace with their women friends. They comment on the ease when traveling with women, how women share domestic duties, how they do not need coddling. Some women even mention how much physical space men take up. They feel free to express their resentment about the way their domestic duties follow them wherever they travel when they are supposed to be "retired." They envy us our female companionship.

After women and men get adjusted to the fact that Irene and I are traveling together, they get very confused and puzzled. Sometimes they learn that we live together. We use terms like "we," "us," "ours" in the same context they do. Sooner or later they come out with the next most often asked question, "You girls are sisters, aren't you?"

NEWFOUNDLAND *December, 1986*

Irene and I lived most of July and August, 1986, in our motorhome exploring Newfoundland, the uniquely beautiful North Atlantic island province of Canada. We loved its rocky coastline, dotted with more than a thousand tiny, picturesque fishing villages, and its tree-covered interior, crisscrossed with a myriad of fish-filled rivers and lakes. Most of the island's half-million people live a rural, family centered life. Its urban centers, St. Johns, with a population of 86,000 (and one Gaymen's bar), Cornerbrook, with 35,000 inhabitants, and Stephenville and Gander, with 10,000 people in each, provide little of what we think of as city-life. Newfoundland, to us, is cool summer weather, wild, rugged terrain, unpolluted, christmas-tree scented air, cod, salmon, moose, bears, and friendly, talkative, unsophisticated people. We found it a wonderful place to visit; but, for Lesbians, Newfoundland is no place to live.

One Sunday afternoon, we were driving along the coastline of a small bay between the towns of Fatima [Our Lady of] and Lourdes [Our Lady of] when we passed a parish churchyard with a summer bazaar in full swing. I know about church bazaars from my old life as a Catholic mother and pillar-of-the-church. I know that where there is a bazaar, there is homemade food for sale. Sure enough, the parish women were serving dinner, giving us the opportunity to try the food that ordinary Newfoundlanders eat. The meal was salt beef, very salty, and very, very boiled potatoes, cabbage, and rutabagas. It was not particularly appetizing. However, the home-made desserts were great and the women were dear. They were curious about us, strangers unusual enough to come all the way from the paradise of Southern California to their rugged, seldom-visited island home.

In the crowded parish dining hall, we spotted a woman seated alone at the end of the long table, one over from the one at which we were seated. Her hair was short and she wore no make-up. She wore jeans and boots, and her shirt was tailored. Many Newfoundland women keep their hair short and wear unisex clothes and no makeup, though not the ones at this church event. But this woman was different. She had that undeniable, impossible to describe, we know

26

it when we see it, Lesbian Look. We made eye contact at once. She looked and smiled, looked and smiled, looked and smiled. Irene and I did the same. Several times she bent her head as if studying the food on her plate, then looked over at us, raised her eyebrows and grinned. "By yourself, I see, Teresa," spoke the priest as he walked past her. "How's your mother?" "Better today," she replied. Her meal was finished, she rose and, avoiding eye contact with us, she quickly left the room.

Now it was obvious to us that she had been thrilled to see two Lesbians in the room, obvious that she wanted us to know our presence pleased her. She could not risk speaking to us though. There was nothing stopping the non-Lesbian women from talking to us, from asking questions, from waving others over to meet us, but external and internal homophobia stopped this Lesbian from treating us as the other women did. Because she could tell we were Lesbians, she feared the others might figure out we were Lesbians too and, seeing her with us, they might guess about her and . . . . We could have wept.

Irene, a Lifelong Lesbian who has been fighting internal and external homophobia for more than forty years, tells me that most places used to be like a dining hall at a church bazaar in Newfoundland. She worries that life for Lesbians could once again be like that of our Newfoundlander sister. . . . The thought makes us shudder.

LOOKING FOR LESBIANS *January, 1984*

Looking for Lesbians is a hobby I share with my companion lover. It is an amusing pastime when we are at home, surrounded by women we know are Lesbians; but when we go traveling the back roads of North America in our motor home, looking for Lesbians becomes serious business. We usually stay in campgrounds in national, state, provincial, and county parks far from urban centers. As a result, we are not able to consult a phone book and then casually drop in at a local women's bookstore, bar, center whenever we need the sight of other Lesbians. We started our RV expedition firm in the belief that "We Are Everywhere!" Over the past four years, we have honed our looking-for-Lesbians skills to a fine art, and to our delight have found us everywhere.

So what does a Lesbian look like? Well, speaking very generally, a Lesbian, when not at work or in costume, looks like a woman for whom bodily comfort when wearing clothes is more important than appearing "attractive," that is, of drawing to one's self the sexual attention of men. Lesbians, generally, seem less elaborately dressed, made-up, coiffed, than other women. In fashion magazines this Lesbian look is called "understated."

So what does a Lesbian look like? I smiled and smiled at a stunning, short-haired woman standing alone at a scenic view pull-off on a Vermont

28

highway. She was wearing highly polished, flat-heeled shoes, a blazer, a tailored silk blouse and sharply-creased pants. She slipped her hands, fingernails short and manicured, into her pockets and smiled back at me. We saw her again when she passed us on the road in a white Cadillac convertible with the top down. I honked and she smiled and waved as she sped by. Irene agreed the woman was a Lesbian and called me a flirt. She knows my fondness for the "blazer dyke" look.

The Lesbian clues here were more subtle than clothing. The fact that this Lesbian did not "soften" the severity of her clothes with a "feminine frill" was encouraging. For us, the clincher was the way she flipped that jacket behind her hip bones in an unmistakable dykely way as she put her hands in her pants pockets.

Checking out shoes when looking for Lesbians is an elimination device, a negative marker. Lesbians wear sensible shoes whenever possible. Irene and I learned to pass right by a woman who looks like a Lesbian from head to ankle, but wears flimsy shoes with pointed toes and heels. She is sure to mention a husband by her second sentence.

So what does a Lesbian look like? Well, we saw two old women drive into a campground in a large motor home. One dog and no men accompanied them. These are Lesbian-positive clues. We seldom see old women in campgrounds unless they are accompanied by old men. They walked the dog, each wearing a long "ladies" winter coat and lipstick. We casually intercepted them.

"Nice dog," says Irene. The dog growled. We mentioned the movie about nuclear war on TV the evening before.

"They should go to Russia. Show it to the Communists," they angrily replied. We walked on. If they were Lesbians, I did not want to know.

"Not Lesbians," pronounced my expert. "There are Lesbians who wear 'ladies' coats and Lesbians who wear lipstick. There are even Lesbians who prefer nuclear war to 'Godless Communism' but Lesbians would not let their dog growl at women without correcting it."

We had better luck with two old women in a pick-up truck pulling a thirty-foot trailer. The dyke driving backed the rig into the campsite next to us in three moves! We walked over to check them out. They were wearing identical jackets adorned with patches from every state park in South Carolina. We admired their trailer; they admired our motor home. We talked about favorite parks.

Then one woman asked, "You two sisters?"

I answered, "No, are you?"

"Nope!" they smiled and invited us for dinner in their thirty-footer. It wasn't more than three sentences later that we were using the "L" word.

In our travels, we frequently see pairs of women who pique our interest. They wear either look-alike backpacks or look-alike boots or shoes, windbreakers or parkas, or all of the above, in the same color, style, or brand. We call it the Lesbian

BobbseyTwins look. We love it. We've met lots of great Lesbians because of it.

At a campground in Maine, we were in the laundry staring at the dryer when a blue van pulled up. It contained two women and one large dog. The woman nearest us was wearing three tiny earrings in one ear and no make up. I started to get excited, but Irene advised caution. She reminded me that the line between Dyke attire and non-Lesbian casual is fuzzy nowadays. The stranger hauled herself out of the van in one large motion. She stood there, in hiking boots and blue jeans, smoothing out the wrinkles in a plaid flannel shirt. When she smiled in that certain way at her similarly clothed companion, Irene admitted we had struck gold. She ambled out of the laundry wearing her WOMEN TAKE BACK THE NIGHT T-shirt and struck up a conversation with the women. Soon, we were enjoying our first four-Lesbian conversation in a month and loving it.

Lesbians can usually be found in the company of other women. Non-Lesbians frequently spend most of their time with women, too. So this is not a clue in and of itself. Refinements are needed.

One warm November day, walking along the path through the sand dunes at Huntington Beach State Park in South Carolina, we saw two women seated on a blanket on the deserted beach. We stood and watched them a minute and knew they were Lesbians. How did we know they were Lesbians? Well, I thought they were Lesbians because they were two women over thirty, seated together while flying a kite. They were not amusing a child. They were not holding the kite for a husband. They were sitting on a beach and flying a kite for their own pleasure, an unlikely activity for non-Lesbians.

"John dear, I am going camping with Mary for a few days so we can bask on the beach and fly kites," she says.

"What a great idea," he says. "Have a good time."

No way!

Irene was sure they were Lesbians when the woman with the kite, wanting to stand up, handed the kite-string holder to the other woman without asking AND without looking to see if she was taking it. They knew we were Lesbians, not because we were two middle-aged women on the beach at a park unaccompanied by children or men. They said they knew because of the intimacy they perceived in our gestures, movements, conversation and activity as we set up our beach space.

Another time we set up camp in a park in Manitoba in sight of a motor home with Florida plates. We watched a woman emerge with a dog on a leash. She was wearing a green and white striped rugby shirt tucked into very tailored cotton pants which were closed with a narrow belt. Her hair was short and her face was make-up free. Irene went out to make conversation using the dog as a pretense. Pretty soon she called me over "to see the dog." Juanita was talkative and kept saying "we" this and "we" that. She did not mention a husband; and her conversation was remarkably free of sex-specific pronouns. We were encouraged. It wasn't long before Ginny stuck her head out the RV door, saw us and came over. She was dressed much like her partner, the Bobbsey Twins again. We had a fine time with them. Like us, they were retired and living full-time on the road.

Of course, all of our Lesbian clues are only partly true, or sometimes true, or for some Lesbians, never true. Irene has been looking for Lesbians for forty years and she still gets fooled -- not in thinking a woman is a Lesbian when she is not -- but in thinking a woman is not a Lesbian when she is. I err in the other direction, assuming women are Lesbians only to have them stroll away, hanging onto the arm of a non-woman.

Still, there is an unmistakable something about Lesbians. Perhaps it is the walk; and I do not mean the Lesbian stomp. The Lesbian walk is a solid placing of the feet on the ground, not a tentative, tippy-toed sway, but the assertively nonchalant stride of a woman who belongs to herself. I have seen Lesbians costumed for work in dresses and high-heels, walking Lesbian. The sight is awe-inspiring.

Along with the walk is a certain stance, a way of moving the body that is Lesbian. Lesbians, generally, move as if the various parts of our bodies, in use at the moment, belong to us, not as if the parts were borrowed from their owners and heaven help us if we bruise anything.

Standing with one's feet apart, rather than with one foot slightly forward, or with one foot carrying most of the weight, is a Lesbian stance. One or both hands in the pockets of pants, especially when wearing a blazer, is a Lesbian stance. More than eight inches of space between the knees when sitting in slacks in public is suspect; crossing one's legs by putting the ankle of one leg on the knee of the other is a dead giveaway!

However, the most telling clue when looking for Lesbians is eye contact. I learned about the eye contact theory from Rita Mae Brown when we first met back in 1975. She said she can tell a woman is a Lesbian when she makes eye contact with her. If the woman looks back, holding contact instead of letting her gaze slide quickly away, she is probably a Lesbian.

"That's not true," I argued. "I usually make eye contact with women; and I am not a Lesbian."

"Hmmmm!" said Rita Mae as she began to laugh.

DEDICATED TO MIDDY[1]
OR THE CAUSES OF LESBIANISM *October , 1983*

One topic non-Lesbians in general, our families in particular, and Lesbians ourselves puzzle over endlessly is the "cause" of Lesbianism. We have a wide array of causes from which to choose the one which suits us. The following is a partial list of some of the more popular causes of Lesbianism I have heard or read about, in no order at all.

1. The no-cause cause. It goes like this. For no apparent reason, about 10% of human females are born with a sexual preference for other females. These females become the female elite or doomed sufferers, depending upon one's point of view. The no-cause cause is especially popular with Lifelong Lesbians who love saying, "I've always been a Lesbian. Don't know why. Just lucky, I guess!" Then they smile. "Ah!"

2. Females whose mothers, in thought, word and deed, are critical of men in general and/or their husbands in particular, grow up to be Lesbians.

3. Females whose mothers, in thought, word and deed are devoted to men in general and/or their husbands in particular, grow up to be Lesbians.

4. Females whose mothers do not love them enough grow up to be Lesbians.

5. Females whose mothers love them too much grow up to be Lesbians.

6. Females whose mothers neglect them in favor of sons grow up to be Lesbians.

These last four causes are variations on the "Lesbians are women who have not outgrown the need for a mother and seek her in their adult relationships." This is considered unhealthy by those who think we should look for a father in our adult relationships.

7. Females whose mothers (or fathers) treat them as the son in the family grow up to be Lesbians.

8. Females who prefer boy toys and sports and activities grow up to be Lesbians.

9. Females who complain about and resent boy privileges -- staying out after dark, mowing lawns instead of babysitting and housework, for example, -- grow up to be Lesbians.

10.Females who excel in "naturally" male activities -- sports, math, science, mechanics, etc. -- grow up to be Lesbians.

These four are variations of the "Lesbians are women who want to be men" cause.

11.Lesbians are women who were molested/raped when young.

12. Lesbians are women who had bad sexual experiences with men.

13. Lesbians are women who cannot get a man.

14. Lesbians are women who are broken-hearted over a man.

These four causes are popular with certain non-Gay men.

Do not tell these men you are a Lesbian. They are likely to take it as a dare.

15. Females immaturely fixated on the clitoris as the center of female pleasure become Lesbians.

16. Females whose lives of heterosexual promiscuity jade them become Lesbians.

17. Females who are frigid become Lesbians.

18. Females who are over-sexed become Lesbians.

19. Females who prefer to live selfish lives of pleasure and self-indulgence instead of ennobling themselves by the sacrifices, hard work and suffering of matrimony and motherhood become Lesbians.

These five causes are popular with non-Lesbian, married women whose lives are filled with hard work, unsatisfying sex, unappreciative husbands and children, and who look forward to happiness in heaven as a reward for the vale of tears they live on earth.

20. And so on. The causes I've missed.

What can we deduce from this? Those of us who are out to our mothers know that mothers believe they are the cause of Lesbianism. Most say, "What did I do wrong?" My mother said that to me, and I was a 43 year old mother and grandmother at the time. A Hindu Lesbian I know said that when she told her mother the good news, the poor woman threw her hands up in the air and cried, "What did I do in my past life to deserve this!"

The point is, no one really knows what causes some girls to resist successfully, and some women to successfully overcome, the constant, lifelong, personal and institutional coercion to live heterosexual lives; and the "cause" one believes in says more about the believer than about Lesbianism.

Most Lesbians, though disagreeing about "causes," do agree with the "experts" that only around 10% of the female population is Lesbian. They see the "natural order" of females to consist of ten percent Lesbians and ninety percent the mostly heterosexual majority. It is this ten to ninety belief which keeps everyone concentrating on the "causes" of Lesbianism. If Lesbianism is the anomaly, the oddity, then a discussion of causes makes sense. But what if Lesbianism, the emotional and sexual attraction of female to female, *is* the natural order, and that of female to male the anomaly?

Let us suppose, for a moment, that females *do* have a natural affinity and attraction for one another, and if free to do so, would couple with males only as a reproductive activity. (This is a logical supposition when one remembers the enormous differences in the physiological sexual responses of females and males documented by Masters and Johnson.) Then let us suppose that males decided it was in their best interests to coerce females to believe and behave as if we have no intrinsic meaning or life in us except through our service to them -- and to hell with the differences in our sexual responses! With the power to do it, men could create a social structure that would 1) deny women sexuality; 2) force male sexuality upon women; 3) command or exploit women's labor to control their production; 4) control and rob women of their children; 5) confine women physically and prevent their movement; 6) use women as objects in male transactions; 7) cramp women's creativeness; 8) withhold from women large areas of the society's knowledge and cultural attainments.[2] This society would be called patriarchy, meaning "men in power." Within this patriarchy, perhaps only ten percent or so of the females would be able to break through the coercion and lies to remember and act upon our natural woman-loving origins. The female majority could then be perceived as a pre-Lesbian, heterosexually coerced, oppressed people!

It is only within this context that we can profitably discuss those situations and activities which facilitate the discovery of one's woman-loving self -- or -- the causes of Lesbianism. If in fact, we do live under a system which coerces the majority of females into the service of males without their *informed consent*, then it becomes the loving duty of those of us who have successfully resisted or escaped from the intimate expression of that service to assist our sisters to do likewise. Increasing the number of Lesbians may not, of itself, bring about the liberation of all women, except as this increases the numbers of women who, in their personal lives at least, learn to feel, think and behave as free women. This goal is a worthy one. Just think, if each Lesbian assists in the discovery of the Lesbian self of only one of the pre-Lesbian women she knows, by next year the female population will be 20% Lesbian![3]

THE LESBIAN AS HERO *March 1983*

When I studied literature in college, I was taught that there are three basic plots, basic conflicts, in literature as in life. These are: man in conflict with nature; man in conflict with society; and man in conflict with himself. There was no talk about "man" really meaning "woman and man." Scholars generally agreed that women and our lives seldom make great literature. They also agreed that women seldom wrote great literature because we were innately incapable of creating anything but babies, or because the subject matter which usually interests women, life from a woman's point of view, is not the stuff of "great" literature, or because women's point of view does not reflect reality accurately, is not "universal." They saw our conflicts as sometimes interesting, but almost never "heroic." In their opinion, man's conflicts create great literature; woman's conflicts produce soap operas. The emergence of women studies programs in colleges and high schools has ameliorated the infallibility of such "scholarly" opinion somewhat; but it is still a dominant assumption of American literature.

The situation is not any better in the other arts or in popular culture. Usually women and our lives are considered not appropriate for high drama, not worthy of serious consideration. We can count the serious books, plays, films, television programs written by women and/or about women and our lives; and those we do have almost always center on the relationships of women with our children and/or our men. In the U.S., even these serious attempts to reflect the real, the true lives of women are quite recent. It is anybody's guess how long we will have to wait to see the lives and conflicts of women as persons, rather than as mothers or as "love interest," represented seriously in art and culture.

(The novel, *The Color Purple*, by Alice Walker, is an example of a brilliant book which takes its woman protagonist seriously in all aspects of her person and in all important relationships of her life. The film, *The Color Purple*, is an example of what the patriarchy can do to such a book. It erased the wholeness of the woman, her spiritual life, her heroism, her sister-love and Lesbian love, and replaced them with sentimentality and slapstick, insulting women and Lesbians, particularly Black women and Black Lesbians, and in general, insulting all Black people and their customs and institutions.)

Women frequently see our lives as others interpret them, and do not believe there is much that is extraordinary about the way we live. Lesbians, for example, are so accustomed to our own lives, so used to Lesbian stories of struggle and sacrifice and courage and perseverance that we do not notice the heroic dimension of these tales. Heroic characteristics are so much a part of Lesbian life that we take them for granted, and look for the inspiration we need in the tales of struggle, sacrifice, perseverance and courage demonstrated by the mostly white, always heterosexual, real and fictional male heroes of our society. Now I am not suggesting these heroes are not inspiring, though most of them don't survive a test for the sexism and racism inherent in their heroism. I am suggesting that it is the Lesbian who ought to be the real, the fictional, and the mythic hero of society.

I believe the Lesbian is the quintessential rebel. Each Lesbian is a person who must be in rebellious conflict with society, and herself, at different times throughout her life, in order to BE herself, as well as to be true to herself. The Lesbian could be the protagonist who inspires humanity to rebel against conformity and oppression, to act with courage and daring in the face of enormous odds because we all do just that. After all, men are *expected* to be heroic, even though they do not all achieve hero status. No matter how great the feats of daring done by men, they cannot compare to the everyday heroism of women in general, and Lesbians in particular. For women to do anything *on our own* is to defy men and their determination that we not act independently, let alone heroically. Lesbians, therefore, are always "marching to a different drummer," always living a "give me liberty or give me death" kind of life. It is the Lesbian who lives the profoundest non-conformity, choosing to live contrary to the heterosexual imperative that is the basic belief of every institution of every social structure of the modern world. What lessons in courage the world could learn from us!

Of course, everyone's favorite heroic conflict has sexual love as its motivating factor. Most "great" love stories center around a man in conflict with his society whose rules deny him access to and/or marriage with the woman he wants; or a man in conflict with some other man who wants the same woman he wants; or a man who is in conflict with himself because he believes it is wrong to want the woman he wants. These are the stories of David and Bathsheba, Lancelot and Guinevere, Abelard and Heloise, Romeo and Juliet, Othello and Desdemona, Cyrano and Roxanne, Tristan and Isolde, the Duke and Duchess of Windsor, Porgy and Bess, Abie and his Irish Rose. These stories are high drama, involving great personal sacrifice, family discord, religious turmoil, social disgrace, banishment, exile and even death. We love these lovers and the poems, plays, operas, novels, and films they have inspired. But even the meekest, mildest, mousiest Lesbian has quietly lived this kind of high drama unnoticed even by herself! In fact, many, if not most Lesbians have defied their families, rebelled against the rules of their religion and their culture, left the place of their birth, experienced or risked societal disgrace, without even knowing if there would ever be a Beloved for them at all.

As for risking all for love, Lesbians have the corner on that market as well. Two women together is the "mixed marriage" par excellence! It matters not that we may both be Catholic or Jewish or Native American or Chinese or disabled, Southerners or rich. Our families will not throw a party and invite the neighbors to witness our rituals. There are no "wedding" presents from the grandparents; no collection at work for a gift. And we cannot hope for a softening of attitudes "when the babies come." When women choose to love other women, we are choosing to risk life-long estrangement from family, neighbors, colleagues, and society at large. And we do not leap off cliffs in dramatic suicide pacts because of such hardships. The truth is that ordinary, everyday Lesbians think the love of women is worth the hardships that are considered extraordinary and awesome and inspiring for women and men who live heterosexual lives. The truth is that these ordinary, everyday Lesbians are so accustomed to those hardships that we seldom think they deserve mention, let alone an opera! I wonder what would happen to all those "star-crossed" love stories if the truth of our Lesbian love stories could be told. With Lesbian visibility might come, not only our liberation, but also a redefinition of rebellion, conformity, courage and some truly inspiring love stories!

WOULD KNOWING THIS
HAVE MADE A DIFFERENCE? *Nov/Dec., 1982*

As we all know, a favorite Lesbian pastime is looking for Lesbians among family members, colleagues, neighbors, and at women's gatherings of every sort. We love to wonder about the Lesbian possibilities of women athletes, politicians, movie stars and all other famous women, especially those we admire. Lesbian historians carry their wonderings further than we do. They have been getting access to the letters and diaries of famous women they have wondered about. As a result of their work, many loving Lesbian sisters have been returned to us.

So! Do you know that one of the most influential women in all the history of the United States was a Lesbian? No, I don't mean Eleanor Roosevelt. She was a Lesbian of course, and Lenore Hickok was certainly not her only Lesbian lover or Lesbian friend. No, no, not Emily Dickinson. Emily was a Lesbian, and we now know that her niece changed the pronouns in her poems to keep us from finding out. But this Lesbian is more influential than the poet. And no, not H.D. or Amy Lowell, even though both of these Lesbians were influential poets, too. She's not Lorraine Hansberry either, though this Lesbian's award-winning play, *Raisin In The Sun*, made theater history. And no, not Rosa Bonheur, the Lesbian famous for her paintings of horses.

No, not Katherine Lee Bates either. She and her lover, Katherine Coman, were important teachers at Wellesley College; and my heart always pitter-pats when I hear "America, The Beautiful," knowing she wrote it. But I don't mean her.

Have you run out of guesses yet? It's not Emily Blackwell, M.D. She was an influential Lesbian, younger sister of Elizabeth Blackwell, the first woman to attend an American medical school. Emily's companion lover was Elizabeth Cushier, by the way. Emily and her older sister co-founded the New York Infirmary for Women and Children, and Emily was the hospital's administrator for all of her professional life. She also founded the Woman's Medical College, training 364 women physicians before merging the school with Cornell University's medical school.

Do you think I mean S. Josephine Baker, M.D.? She was influential, I'll admit. Dr. Baker was a pioneer in public health. She set up tax-supported community health centers, well-baby clinics, classes in maternal and infant health care and nutrition in New York City. Her work reduced the city's infant mortality rate from 111 to 66 per 1,000 live births by the time she retired in 1923, the lowest achieved in any major city in the U.S. or Europe at that time. Other cities adopted her programs, too. S. Josephine Baker was a Lesbian (her companion lover was also a physician), whose life made a difference to a lot of people; but she is not the Lesbian I have in mind.

Jane Addams is the Lesbian I mean. She and her first companion lover, Ellen Starr, founded America's first settlement house, Hull House. Jane had the vision, and Ellen had the connections. Between them, they drew young women and old money to Hull House to improve the living conditions of Chicago's immigrant population and to give meaning to the lives of the women doing Hull House work. Hull House was Jane's home for the rest of her life, Ellen's home until her conversion to Catholicism in 1920, and the residence of most of the women who worked there.

By 1893, Hull House was the center for forty community organizations and projects, and its buildings included a cooperative boarding house for working women, day care center, dispensary, playground, gymnasium, cooking and sewing school, music school and concert hall, art gallery, and little theater. Over two thousand people used its facilities every month. Hull House became the model for all other settlement houses in America during the period from 1889 to the end of the first world war, not just in its services, but also in its philosophy. This was no group of "Lady Bountifuls" helping the downtrodden masses. Jane instilled in the women the conviction that the interaction between the privileged women and the oppressed immigrants was of more benefit to the privileged than it was to the oppressed.The Hull House philosophy and its direct services were only part of its work and influence however. Every problem Hull House was alleviating became a public issue by the conscious activity of these women. They did scholarly research on the "problem." They published their results. They lectured, organized mass meetings, demonstrated, enlisted the liberals and the press and sympathetic politicians in the cause, put their expertise at the service of the immigrant groups and Black organizations working with them. Then they wrote the legislation needed to correct the "problem," lobbied for its passage, and frequently were appointed by government to organize and/or administer the new program, policy or agency. In this too, Hull House was the model for crusading women, many of them Lesbians, in its sister settlement houses across America.

Jane Addams' counterpart in New York City was Lillian Wald who, with the companion lover of her youth, Mary Brewster, founded the Henry Street Settlement House on the lower East Side of the city in 1893. The women from both houses and those living and working in similar establishments throughout the country, formed an informal social and professional network. They shared ideas, strategies, expertise. They traveled together, vacationed together, lived in each other's establishments when affairs of work or the heart moved them. Many of these women became very famous. They were reviled or admired, called communists or saints, received high honors in their old age, died and were erased from the memory of the American people. Only their creative and innovative achievements live on, although these too go unnoticed because it is not brought to public attention that these innovations did not always exist, that some WOMEN/some LESBIANS thought them up and saw to it they became a reality. These are some examples: Immigrant leagues and protective legislation; state and national factory and sweatshop health and safety legislation; Public Health Nursing; child labor laws; separation of children and adults in jails, mental hospitals and other public institutions; the Visiting Nurses Program; juvenile courts; departments of probation; compulsory school attendance; non-segregated public schools in Chicago; ungraded public school classes for slow and mentally retarded children; minimum wage legislation; consumer protection laws; inclusion of art and music programs in public schools; the Public School Nursing Programs; social work as a profession; the case work method of public welfare systems; federal grants-in-aid to states to combat infant and maternal death and disease; national and international committees to publicize and stop the traffic in women and children; nursing programs for industrial workers; establishment of nursing programs in colleges and universities; the National Children's Bureau.

Hull House and Henry Street activists were founding members of:

American Civil Liberties Union; the National Association for the Advancement of Colored People; the National Consumers League; the Women's Party; and Women's International League for Peace and Freedom.

They were active in local, state, national, and international women's suffrage organizations as well.

Jane Addams was a hugging and kissing and sexually active Lesbian, insisting upon double bed accommodations at hotels for herself and her companion lovers. In 1931, JANE ADDAMS WAS AWARDED THE NOBEL PEACE PRIZE! How's that for a Lesbian success story!

Would knowing all this have made a difference in our Lesbian lives? Just imagine telling our mothers, "Mom, I know you'll be pleased to learn that I am a Lesbian," and then having to deal with her expectations of us as potential Nobel Prize winners!

PS. *Non-Lesbians may not agree about a Lesbian identity for some of the Lesbians listed above. They are entitled to their opinion, but we know they often do not recognize a Lesbian when they see one.*

THINKING ABOUT BISEXUALITY
February 1984

When I think, talk, write about women who are not Lesbians, I try to use the terms non-Lesbian, pre-Lesbian, women who live heterosexual lives. I try to avoid saying heterosexual woman. This is not a bit of Lesbian cleverness on my part. Instead, it is an attempt at clear thinking, an example of words expressing real life as I experience it. I think we err when we label a woman heterosexual in a world 1) where all women are presumed, expected, and mentally, physically, emotionally, spiritually and economically coerced to live heterosexual lives; 2) where compulsory heterosexuality is the principal organizing institution of personal life; 3) where the heterosexual model of woman serving man is the model for all public relationships between women and men; 4) where living outside of the institution of heterosexuality is A) unthinkable or, if thought of is B) taught as disgusting, sinful, sick and no fun at all or if acted upon, is C) punished by secrecy or social ostracism and loss of the civil rights and legal protections afforded citizens of the nation.

Given this enormous pressure on women to live heterosexual lives, we cannot say, "most women are heterosexual," and mean anything comparable to saying, "some women are Lesbians." In the first place, heterosexuality is not a sexual preference for most women. They do not know there is an agreeable alternative to men as love objects, sex partners, life companions. They do not prefer and/or choose men, except as an alternative to those known and abhorred states called spinsters and old maid.

Neither is heterosexual an aspect of the psycho-social identity of most women who live heterosexual lives. When asked to give words which define who they are, most women do not include heterosexual, and for the same reason that most white people would not include white in their definition. Of course, if the question was asked by a woman known to be a Lesbian, they would be more likely to say heterosexual.

Lesbian, on the other hand, is both a conscious sexual and affectional preference and an important component of the psycho-social identity of women who love other women. Lesbians know they can marry and live unhappily ever after as so many women do. Instead we choose to live outside compulsory heterosexuality because the desire to act upon our preference for women as love objects, sex partners and life companions is stronger than the fear of the negative social consequences of our actions.

Because of the negative social stigma attached to Lesbianism however, Lesbians usually experience a time of internal struggle in order to accept our Lesbian self and our Lesbian group membership. The Lesbian identity forged from this struggle is so important that it ranks in the top two or three defining characteristics: I am a Black Lesbian; I am a Lesbian mother; I am a disabled Lesbian, and so forth. Hence our use of the terms Lesbian and non-Lesbian is logical.

However, what are we to think when women say they are bisexual? We must admit that when a woman says she is bisexual most Lesbians do not believe her. We think she is pre-Lesbian, in transition, going through a bisexual phase on her journey to Lesbianism. We think she is protecting herself from her Lesbian fears. Most of us feel more or less protective of women we think are in this bisexual place, especially when we know they are not seeing men. All Lesbians know women who used to be "bisexual," including, for some, themselves.

Our disbelief in bisexuality works to women's advantage, regardless of how personally annoying it is to them. Our disbelief insures their inclusion in the Lesbian sub-culture.

Sometimes, however, this disbelief takes a harsher expression, with Lesbians calling some women's bisexuality a cop-out, a way of profiting from their inclusion in the camaraderie and richness of the Lesbian community, in addition to the joys of women-loving -- without accepting the individual and societal penalties that "real" Lesbians suffer.

I do not accept the premise that bisexual women are penalized in straight society. We know that non-women find the idea of Lesbian sex a turn-on, and find the bisexual women who do it, sexy! We also know that female bisexuality is considered a phase there, too. And we, too, expect women like these to go back to men permanently when it is advantageous to do so, and to take their "sexy Lesbian stories" back with them.

These responses to bisexual women also come from the real life experiences of Lesbians. In addition, they come from the Lesbian inability to believe that any woman could feel sexually and emotionally attracted to women and men with equal intensity.

In my opinion, bisexuality cannot logically be called a sexual/affectional preference. Some women who say they are bisexual insist that the gender of their lovers is irrelevant to them, that they do not choose lovers on the basis of gender. Some even criticize Lesbians who choose to avoid relationships with, and/or who question the choices of women who continue to relate intimately with non-women. They say we are intolerant, bigoted, Falwellish for considering the gender of our partners important, as if compulsory Lesbianism were the organizing societal institution of personal life. Their attitude trivializes, erases the real oppression experienced by Lesbians for their women-loving.

Some women who say they are bisexual say the gender of their lovers is important, though they say they do not prefer one sex over the other. They say they are attracted to women for our similarities and to non-women for their differences from themselves. Some say that physical differences of women and men as sexual partners make their sexual lives more exciting. Some find that the differing ways women and men relate to them personally add something extra to their lives.

I think that when a woman who calls herself bisexual goes to the movies and then to bed with a man for whom she feels lust and affection, a man whose company she enjoys, whose attention she hopes to encourage, with whom she is sharing life stories, dreams, aspirations, she is living a conscious heterosexual life. She may call herself bisexual, but she is doing what she was socialized to do. Like most women in the world, she is giving love, attention, respect, companionship and service to a person who profits from the personal and institutional oppression of women, including herself. The fact that she may expect or demand respect and reciprocity from the man, and may receive it, does not alter the material reality of the heterosexual "normality" of her situation.

While this woman is consciously living a heterosexual life and calling herself bisexual, she enjoys the privileges which accrue to those who conform to the sexual standards of their society. In this instance, the woman, at the very least, enjoys the freedom to hold hands, snuggle against, even kiss her male partner while in line outside the movie theater, without the risk of job loss, ridicule or physical injury.

In addition, women who consciously relate to men know they may become emotionally engaged with a man deeply enough to make a long-term commitment to him. They live the possibility of becoming half of a "legitimate" couple, of being able to discuss his foibles with his mother, of taking him to work-related social events without risk of punishment or sanctions.

On the other hand, I think that when a woman who calls herself bisexual goes to the movies and then to bed with a woman for whom she feels lust and affection, a woman whose company she enjoys, whose attention she hopes to encourage, with whom she is sharing life stories, dreams, aspirations, she is not living a Lesbian life, nor does she have a Lesbian consciousness of her experience. The experience of her chosen heterosexual yesterday and the possibility of a chosen heterosexual tomorrow keeps her always

relating to Lesbians and to Lesbianism as a heterosexual woman who sometimes relates to/has sex
with women.

Women who call themselves bisexual and actively relate to women and men certainly have
the right to live as they please. However, they do
not have the right to expect Lesbians to accept
them as "one of us," or to approve or applaud
their choice of men as partners, even now and
then. After all, there is nothing new, original or
avant garde about relating to men, and the refusal
of Lesbians to do so is the basis for our oppression.

All of the above leaves us with a logical para-
dox. Women who call themselves bisexual -- not
because they are in transition or are afraid of their
Lesbianism -- but because they choose to relate
sexually to both women and men, are the only
women who are really heterosexual. They are the
only women who choose to relate to men after
having known and experienced our non-compul-
sory alternative.

IN THE PRESENCE OF GREATNESS:
Barbara Deming *December, 1984*

Because we had friends in common who insisted we meet, Barbara Deming invited my
companion lover and me to visit her at her home
on Sugarloaf Key when our RV trip took us to the
Florida Keys in February, 1984. All we knew of
Barbara at the time we received the invitation

was that she was a peace activist, a writer and a Lesbian who was convalescing from a painful and debilitating kidney ailment. We obtained her book, *Remembering Who We Are* and read it aloud over morning coffee on our way south, learning some of who she was and how she thought. We were very impressed by the person revealed in the book. Still, we were reluctant to intrude on a stranger, especially one who was ailing, even though our intrusion would be minimal. We would park in her yard; live in our camper; stay only one night.

Nothing, really nothing could have prepared us for Barbara Deming. To be in her presence was to be in the presence of greatness. She was what some would call an "old soul." I had to fight the urge to kneel, an ingrained Catholic reflex. Joan of Arc came to mind and stayed there -- for both of us. We opened our camper door at her knock. "Hello! I'm Barbara. May I come in?" And her spirit entered our space before her body did. We consciously had to force ourselves to behave in an ordinary way so as not to embarrass ourselves or our extraordinary guest. I have few "new" words or similes to describe our experience of Barbara Deming and find myself falling back on those of my Catholic past. All those stories of angels and saints whose holiness shines through their faces and hands, causing awe and reverence in the hearts of those who saw them reverberated in my mind each time I was in Barbara's presence.

Barbara climbed into our camper that first afternoon swathed in sweaters and coat, muffler and gloves, hat and boots. "I can't seem to get warm," she explained, this sixty-seven year old, tall, bone-thin woman with her glowing saint's face. So we talked first about her health, with Irene, a nurse, urging her to eat for strength and to see a traditional physician, "just in case." We talked of Lesbian life; she and Irene pleased to meet another Lifelong Lesbian, to discuss the differences feminism made in their lives. She wanted to know about our work, Califia Community, the **Lesbian News**, my writing. She asked our opinion, our views, on issues she was thinking about. She listened to us with her entire person at attention. The intensity with which she listened left us feeling that what we said was important to her, that we were important to her, that we were important. When she began to tire, she reached out her hands and grasped ours. "I've loved our talk," she said. "You will stay, at least a few days, so we can talk again, won't you?" Since we would have accompanied her to the court of the French Dauphine, we easily agreed to change our plans.

Barbara's place, in a sparsely populated area on Sugarloaf Key, was a small Lesbian enclave, four plain houses surrounded by greenery, trees, shrubs, flowering plants, giving the place a secluded atmosphere. Here she lived with her beloved companion, her Lesbian neighbors, and a constant and ever-changing stream of visitors, strangers like Irene and me, and her friends and comrades from the civil rights, peace and women's liberation movements. Because Barbara was there, the place seemed shot with magic. I wanted my children with me, my sisters, my mother, my friends. I wanted to share this experience with all the people I cared about.

That sharing is impossible now. Barbara died on August 2, 1984. Memorial services were held for her in many places in the east. Friends are writing and publishing moving accounts of the passionate way she lived her dying. Yet few Lesbians know of her life, her work, her books. Barbara Deming? Who was she? She was a powerful woman, a shaper of American society, a LESBIAN whose life and work and words could be a source of pride and inspiration to her Lesbian sisters. She could be lost to us because of sexism and homophobia and the resultant difficulty Lesbians encounter when we try to make ourselves known to one another.

Barbara Deming was born in 1917, the daughter of a well-to-do Republican attorney and a woman of privilege. She attended a private Quaker school through high school. She studied literature and theater at Bennington College. She worked in a variety of jobs related to literature and the theater, including one as film analyst for a Library of Congress project housed at New York City's Museum of Modern Art. She was an aspiring writer. Most of her work of that period was not published until later, but several of her pieces appeared in magazines like **CHARM** and **THE NEW YORKER**. She traveled extensively, too. Her life through her mid-thirties, as it appeared on the surface, could have been a film starring Katherine

Hepburn as the earnest, attractive, dedicated-to-the-single-life career woman, needing only Cary Grant or Spencer Tracy to give her a happy ending.

Barbara was a Lesbian however, rejecting, by sixteen years of age, a traditional life. She learned early to question the so-called truths of her sex, her race, her class, her entire culture. She developed into an American liberal, a Democrat, in favor of civil rights and unions, against racism and the loyalty oath. She was, in fact, similar to the Lesbians of her race, class and generation we know. She might have stayed "ordinary", for a Lesbian, if she had not studied the writing of the Mahatma Gandhi after a trip to India in the fifties. "I realized I was in the deepest part of myself a pacifist," she wrote. She committed herself to non-violent activism and was to become the foremost white spokesperson for non-violence as the sane and ethical way to live one's life and to bring about peace, racial justice and women's liberation.

From 1960 until her death, Barbara lived her truth..."The truth, above all, that every human being deserves respect. We assert the respect due ourselves, when it is denied, through noncooperation; We assert the respect due all others, through our refusal to be violent." This truth took her to Moscow, Cuba, Vietnam in the cause of peace. It succored her during her many imprisonments in the jails of her own country for acts of civil disobedience during demonstrations for peace and racial justice. It gave her the strength for her fasts; and it enabled her to endure the physical and verbal abuse to which she was subjected by the racists and warmongers on the streets, by the Internal Revenue Service, by the House Un-American Activities Committee, and by the former husband of her beloved companion in the courts and in person. Her truth, as she lived it, made Barbara the kind of person who could listen intensely to each person. It was that quality that illustrated the depth of her respect for each person. She would not only risk her life and go to jail for us; she was also willing to listen to the least of us with the attention she gave to those with the power of life and death over the whole human race.

Barbara Deming's written work is known and cherished by thousands of women and men who do not know she was a Lesbian, or who are "shocked" to learn she was a Lesbian, or who admire her "even though" she was a Lesbian. These are the people who write "respectful" obituaries and articles in major newspapers, obituaries and articles which erase her Lesbianism from her life and who will erase it from the history of the non-violent movements for peace and racial justice in our time. This erasure is the final violence done to her; it is the removal of her sexuality when she is no longer here to protest the outrage.

We, her Lesbian sisters, know that her sexuality is likely to be the place from which she grasped the truth by which she lived. Once, when her Lesbianism was under attack she wrote, "In short, my pride was for the first time, perhaps, assaulted

IN ITS DEPTH. One's sexuality...is so at the heart, the heart of one. And just as one fears physical hurt to that part of one's body, feels its vulnerability, so one fears the psychic assault--and of course, yes, precisely because it is most deeply joined to what is spiritual in us, what allows us to lose the cramped sense of being only single selves." And again,". . .because .I am a homosexual I know in my deepest being what it feels like to be despised." It becomes the pleasure, the privilege and the responsibility, of Barbara's Lesbian sisters to remember she is one of us, and to make sure her Lesbian life is not erased from history. Those of us who do not already know her, can meet her in her books. [4]

One last letter was written by Barbara Deming to all of her sisters twelve days before her death. It is her last gift to us.

To so many of you:
I have loved my life so very much and I have loved you so very much and felt so blessed at the love you have given me. I love the work so many of us have been trying to do together and had looked forward to continuing this work, but I just feel no more strength in me now and I want to die. I won't lose you when I die and I won't leave you when I die. Some of you I have most especially loved and felt beloved by and I hope you know that even though I haven't had the strength lately to reach out to you. I love you. Hallowed be (may all be made whole). I want you to know, too, that I die happy.

[1]Middy was a friend, an old woman, a Lesbian since she fell in love with a classmate in the third grade due to cause #1, she told me. She died of cancer recently. I miss her.

[2]These are the eight characteristics of male power in archaic and contemporary societies listed by Kathleen Gough in her article, "The Origin of the Family," in *Toward An Anthropology of Women*, ed. Rayna (Rapp) Reiter, (New York: Monthly Review Press, 1975), pp. 69-70, cited in "Compulsory Heterosexuality and Lesbian Existence," by Adrienne Rich, *Signs*, (Summer 1980)

[3]For readers wanting to read more about Lesbianism from perspectives similar to mine, I recommend the Rich article above, Lillian Faderman's *Surpassing the Love of Men*, (New York: William Morrow and Company, Inc., 1981). Sheila Jeffreys' *The Spinster and Her Enemies*, (Boston: Pandora Press, 1985). Marilyn Frye's *The Politics of Reality*, (Freedom, California: The Crossing Press, 1983) and dozens of others available from our women's bookstores.

[4]A good place to start is her last one, a collection of the best pieces from all her previous work. The volume includes information about her life and her political evolution by its editor, Jane Meyerding, and a wonderful introduction by Barbara Smith of Kitchen Table Press. Its title is *We Are All Part of One Another: A Barbara Deming Reader*.

II. The Voices of Experience:
How to live and how to die

PUTTING WOMEN FIRST *November, 1987*

Back in the '60s and '70s, those good old, bad old days of the Women's Liberation Movement, the term "politically correct" was taken very seriously. Generally speaking, those of us who thought of ourselves as members of the WLM (the radicals) evolved a loose set of what we considered politically correct guidelines based principally on our consciousness-raising group experiences. The pre-eminent politically correct behavior for WLM feminists, especially the Lesbians, was to put women first in all things in order to empower women to break the chains -- psychic and material -- that bound us to patriarchy.

We thought big in those days. We believed that equality with men under the laws of the United States of America would not bring about the liberation of all women. Rather, we understood that we were attempting to change attitudes, beliefs, and actions, both personal and institutional, that have oppressed women -- and warped men -- for thousands of years. We were trying to re-invent the world we lived in, without knowing how to do it, so we didn't want to waste our limited resources on whatever did not further our liberation.

I don't want to give the impression that this process was smooth. We were all a jumble of political correctness and incorrectness. Ideas and insights were erupting so rapidly that we couldn't keep up with everything at once. As we sorted things out, we came to some basic ideas that many of us considered essential to the work of women's liberation. Through the process of consciousness-raising, in small, women-only groups, we told our lives to each other and identified the forms and connections of our oppression. Then we set out to remedy our situation. Political correctness was one measure by which we analyzed the problem and the means and behavior we employed to try to solve it.

In C-R groups, we learned that women need women-only groups in order to speak of, and thereby free themselves from, the humiliation, shame, guilt and secrets we are burdened with. We learned that we needed women-only groups, free from the presence of our oppressors, to rid ourselves of our internalized oppression, to unravel the system of lies, distortions and man-serving assumptions that keep us ignorant of our oppression and colluding with it. We learned that we needed to learn we were powerful (could become powerful) by doing things with other women that we feared doing alone. (When attending my first women-only Women's Liberation gathering in 1969, I saw five amazons carry a man, kicking and yelling, out of the auditorium. I'll never forget that sight.)

We learned that even the good men, those with the best of intentions, monopolized, pontificated, undermined, patronized, interrupted and disrupted groups organized to work for the liberation of women. We learned from experience that consciously chosen woman-only space and time was essential to the liberation of women, and therefore, was politically correct.

For some women, it was a short step from woman-only space and time to believing that we cannot empower women to achieve our liberation by working within the system. They said we needed to develop our own, alternative systems which can respond to our needs and aspirations because only we, women/Lesbians, know what it is we need.

Because of our C-R experiences, we believed discussion of a problem, with all women participating, until we reached some consensus, was empowering for women, as well as more likely to result in creative solutions. We believed that rotating jobs and "leadership" positions did the same. We wanted knowledge shared, too.

Since empowering women was a goal as well as a means for us, we believed it was politically correct to conduct our business in this way. We believed that hierarchical structures, decision-making boards, parliamentary procedures might seem efficient in the short run, but, over time, would re-create patriarchy (the "We-know-what-is-best-for-you.-We-can't-trust-the-masses" mentality) in our organizations. We believed the means was as important as the ends, and, in some cases, was the end.

The Women's Liberation Movement's politically correct guidelines of putting women first, women-only spaces and times, and non-hierarchical group process, and the attitudes, behaviors and decisions flowing from them, were constantly under discussion and attack, both within the Movement and outside of it.

Men, of course, hated it all, but disagreements with men, while painful, didn't hurt like the ones we had with our sisters. Sometimes "political correctness" was used as an excuse for personal attacks that destroyed the reputation, the spirit and the projects of countless women. Sometimes, we simply did not know how to disagree politically without taking it personally. Of course, some women love an opportunity to feel self-righteous, and our movement has had its share of them.

This misuse doesn't mean there was something wrong with having guidelines for political correctness. I believe we didn't understand those personal attacks, whether we were the attacker or the target, because we didn't know the extent of our internalized woman-hatred/self-hatred, didn't know how "natural" it is to blame women for disclosing men's crimes against us.

Back then, we didn't understand the phenomenon of "horizontal hostility," which is the sorry truth that oppressed people take their anger and frustration and feelings of powerlessness out on each other. We didn't realize that our horizontal hostility would sometimes keep us from supporting each other or working together to overthrow our oppression. Knowing what I know now about the damage we have suffered at the hands of men and their institutions, I am more impressed than ever about all we accomplished.

Nowadays, some Lesbian feminists respond with laughter, derision and scorn to the term "politically correct." I like to think that most of these women are new enough to Lesbian feminist politics to be unaware of the meaning and history of the concept within the Women's Liberation Movement. I choose to believe most Lesbian feminists are trying to be politically correct without realizing it and could find the concept useful in what seems to me is a resurgence of feminist activism in the Lesbian community.

I know that the visible Lesbian community was created by thousands of unknown Lesbians who put women first, who believed passionately in woman-only space and time, and who suffered through thousands of hours of meetings and unpaid work in hopes of making a difference in the lives of Lesbians coming after them.

THANKSGIVING DAY *November, 1988*

When I think of Thanksgiving Day I feel warmly nostalgic. It is the only holiday I remember from my childhood that was not marred either by poverty or by my parents' work schedules. They always managed to be off work on Thanksgiving Day afternoon or evening; and they always managed to buy a turkey. So even though we did not have company for Thanksgiving Day dinner, we felt good about celebrating the holiday the way we thought everybody else did.

I enjoyed the Thanksgiving Day holiday when my sisters and I were the mothers of small children, too. There was the noise and work of putting on a feast for a crowd, and the cleaning up afterwards, but mostly it was worth it. We were thankful for many things then, including our ability to celebrate the holiday even more like everybody else than our parents did.

When I was a child living in New York City, I participated in many school programs about the first thanks-giving celebration of the Pilgrims and their Indian "friends." I thought the story romantic and the Indians romantic as well. I identified with the Pilgrims, of course.

When my children were in Thanksgiving programs in grade school, I knew little more about Indians or about the relations between Indian and Pilgrim than I did as a child. I was living in Tulsa, Oklahoma, then and knew many people, including my children's father, who said they were "part Indian." They did not "look like" Indians, did not have "Indian" names, did not live on Indian reservations, and so far as I knew they, like me, identified with the Pilgrims during Thanksgiving programs.

I thought I knew "real" Indians -- Tonto/Jay Silverheels, for example, and Jeff Chandler and Debra Paget and Anthony Quinn, and Jennifer Jones and the multitudes of nameless "Indians" in the hundreds of western movies I saw. Indeed, that was the primary way I learned about Indians, from the movies. These Indians, like the ones in the Thanksgiving Day programs, lived a long, long time ago in the romantic past of this country's history. Even the few times I heard of injustices done the Indians, such as the forced relocation of several southeastern tribes to Oklahoma, the events were retold in the past tense. Real Indians were people from the past to me, just like Pilgrims were.

Then, in 1965 when I was 33 years old, I moved to California, college and consciousness. I began to realize how little I knew about everything, including Native Americans. It may seem impossible to younger readers that an intelligent, adult American could be unaware of the existence of millions of living, breathing American Indians in her presence, but I was that ignorant. I was the product of an education, both in my schools and in my culture, designed to make me a non-questioning, faithful, believing citizen of the United States of America (and the same kind of Roman Catholic, but that's another story). As a result, I was shocked when living, breathing American Indians began appearing on my college campus, and everywhere else, demanding their rights. Rights? Where had they come from, these people from my country's past and the motion picture screen? And since they were here, what was the problem about their rights? It's not as if they were Black, the only Americans I knew of who were treated unjustly. Certainly Native Americans, of all people, were citizens, were born here. Didn't they have rights and privileges equal to those of all other American citizens including myself?

Well, that was a long time ago in my personal history, a time when I thought of myself as a "person," an "American," a thoughtful "citizen" who actively supported the Black civil rights movement as the completion of my country's noble experiment in democracy. I thought "We the people" meant me and everyone else except Black Americans, and "we" were working on that oversight. My education inside and outside the college classroom since then continues to change me and my behavior in ways both profound and mundane. Among a host of other things, I have had to change my attitude and behavior towards Thanksgiving Day.

If I were a Native American citizen, would I spread a feast and invite my family and friends to join me in celebrating the survival of the first English colony on my land? Would I invite a Native American to join me in such a celebration? How can I participate in a cultural cover-up designed to make non-Native Americans feel good about our inhuman treatment of Native Americans even as we continue to profit by the injustices done them in the past and in the present? Native Americans are still the economically poorest ethnic group in the country, with the most inadequate health and education services of all Americans. Their land rights, their fishing rights, their mineral rights are still being abridged. They are still being forcibly relocated from their land. Their lives are attacked, insulted, ridiculed and undermined by the personal and institution-alized racism of those non-Native Americans who get misty-eyed and patriotic each Thanksgiving Day. So the fact that they've been able to vote lately and no longer have their chil-dren routinely removed from their homes and placed in "Indian" schools, has not caused them to feel particularly thankful for the Pilgrim suc-cess. The traditional Thanksgiving Day celebra-tion adds insult to their injuries.

The adoption by many counter-culture white Americans -- hippies and Lesbians for example -- of some of the more "interesting/colorful/excit-ing/meaningful" spiritual practices of a variety of Native American tribes amuses some and enrages other tribal people. Native American Lesbians, who experience the active and passive racism of the rest of us, are particularly upset by the specta-cle of Lesbians "playing Indian:" pipe ceremonies, medicine wheels, dances and chants, sweat huts and visions. Such behavior is called Cultural Imperialism, the adoption of some of the practices indigenous to a subject people by their oppressors for the benefit or the enjoyment of the oppressors. By taking up some of the spiritual practices of peo-ple completely absent from our everyday life, with whom we have little or no personal contact, we are able to idealize them, taking what we want from them, like the Pilgrims did, then turning them into symbols and relieving ourselves of the responsibility for our personal and collective racism.

European colonists were surprised and confused by the absence of private property mentality among Native Americans they encountered. They were willing to take what they wanted from a people who didn't believe in ownership, but they did not approve of Native Americans taking from them in return. Hence, the derogatory term, "Indian giver," became part of our vocabulary of ethnic insults.

The Europeans were surprised by some Native Americans' divisions of labor, too. Often these "gentlemen" saw Native American women performing what they considered "men's work": plowing fields, riding horses astride, curing hides, building houses. They were appalled by the work the Native American men "let their women" do and, in coining the term "squaw," created a racial slur for any woman who does heavy, unremitting labor -- like an "Indian wife." They named the child of a European father and a Native American mother "half-breed." They gave us the racial slurs, "She lets her children run around like 'wild Indians'" and "He holds his liquor like a 'drunken Indian.'" And what do we mean when we call cosmetics "warpaint"?

How unthinkingly we perpetuate the racism in the notion that Columbus "discovered" America, and De Soto "discovered" the Mississippi River and so on, as if it took the presence of white men to make geography real!

So what can we non-Native Americans do on Thanksgiving Day? We can be thankful for a four-day weekend and perhaps think about and talk about the ways American Indians and their history and their cultures have been distorted and/or erased from our consciousness and our lives. We can promise ourselves to pay attention to news about Native American affairs in our press and the national media. We can renew our resolve to eliminate racism from our vocabulary and to interrupt it in the speech and behavior of others. We can begin to think about American Indians as girls who sometimes play basketball or need abortions or grow up to be Lesbians -- whatever will help us think of them as people instead of "The Native American," symbol of ecology and spirituality. We can write to Pope John Paul, c/o The Vatican, Rome, Italy, and demand he stop the canonization proceedings of Junipero Serra, the Franciscan priest who brought to California's Native Americans the Catholic missions and the disease, deprivation and death which annihilated them. Then we can have a party and enjoy a happy celebration of Autumn.

HITLER'S BIRTHDAY *June, 1990*

Gainesville, Florida, is the prettiest small city I've ever seen. The streets, even in poor neighborhoods, are tree-lined, live oak, pine, palm, chinaberry, and more flowering trees per capita than any other place in America. It is home to the main campus of the University of Florida. The center of town is the well-preserved historic district, with outdoor cafes edging the cobble-stoned square. Lots of Lesbians live in Gainesville and the surrounding countryside. Irene and I go there for cultural events. We attended a performance of *Dos Lesbos* there, and a reading by May Sarton. Gainesville is a "hip" town.

Our neighbors, Myriam Fougere and Lin Daniels, went to Gainesville last Saturday to see the Lesbians who are silk-screening the T-shirts for the East Coast Lesbians' Festival which they are organizing. When they stopped in the city's historic Square for lunch, they found themselves facing a swastika-draped platform peopled by a group of 16 neo-Nazis staging a rally for Hitler's birthday. They joined the crowd of 200-some anti-Nazi demonstrators, noting that just about all of them were men. A few were members of a Gay group and the rest were mostly leftists. When the rally started, three Nazi women walked to the microphones and addressed the crowd. Immediately, the demonstrators began to shout. "DYKE," they yelled. "CUNT," they roared. "WHORE," they shouted. (The Gaymen did not yell, "DYKE.") Lin and Myriam were horrified. "I'm a dyke," Lin yelled, trying to get the attention of the men. "Call them FASCIST. That's what they are." One man snarled, "Isn't it enough that I'm here demonstrating?" Others agreed. "Yeah! Yeah!" They returned to their shouting and fist-waving, leaving our friends near to tears of anger and frustration.

Those feelings intensified when a leftist woman handed them a flyer. It was a copy of an article that looked like it came from *The National Inquirer*. "WW2's most bizarre secret .... ADOLPH HITLER WAS A WOMAN!" The piece was illustrated by a large drawing of Hitler in a dress and high heeled shoes. "ARTIST'S concept of how Nazi-Germany's Fuhrer might have looked had he dressed like the woman he was." Myriam and Lin cried out, "You can't give these out. It's an insult to women, to you, to us. Is this the worst thing you can say about Hitler? Call him a WOMAN! " The woman smiled meekly and continued to hand out the flyers. "NO! NO!", our friends insisted as they grabbed the stack of flyers and walked away. Lin was crumpling them and throwing them on the ground as she walked. A policeman, alerted by the demonstrators, stopped her. "She has a right to hand them out," he insisted over her protests. She held on tightly when the policeman tried to take the flyers away from her. Finally, threatened with jail, she relented. Myriam then slipped quietly away with her stack and deposited them in a trash bin. And all the while, the men continued their angry "anti-Nazi" chant. "DYKE! CUNT! WHORE!"

The event left Lin and Myriam distraught. "Gaymen and Leftists are supposed to be our *allies*! They are the "good guys!" They hate us too!" They were particularly disturbed because they were forced, by the demonstrators' woman-hating, to empathize and sympathize with the women on the platform, in spite of their Nazi politics. Myriam and Lin are "out" everywhere, so they've had their share of angry men shouting "DYKE! CUNT! WHORE!" at them. Had the male Nazis been the speakers, they know the demonstrators would have attacked the speakers' politics, *not their sex.* "Fascist!" not "Prick!" They also know that as long as men use *woman* and words that signify our femaleness, such as *cunt, dyke, bitch, whore*, as insults, as hate epithets, no woman is exempt from becoming an object of their wrath.

So where were Gainesville's women/Lesbian activists while all this woman-hating was going on? Hundreds of them were demonstrating in front of a newly-opened movie theater on the other side of town. It seems the assistant manager of the theater raped a woman employee. When she reported the rape to the police, four other women employees disclosed his sexual harassment of them. The theater's home company then fired the rape victim, pending the outcome of the investigation, and put the other four on leave without pay until such time as the rape victim "reconsiders" her charge.

The rapist has not been fired or put on leave pending. . .!

When Lin and Myriam returned home to our tiny Lesbian community, they came over to our cottage to tell us what had happened. "How lucky we are to live in woman-only space," sighed Myriam. "And how lucky our Center visitors are to vacation here," commented Irene, noting all the Lesbians in the pool. Lin said their resolve to keep the East Coast Lesbians' Festival a woman-only event was strengthened by their experience. Then they strolled hand-in-hand down Lezzie Lane toward the ocean, hoping to soothe their woman spirits by wading in the water as they watched for dolphins.

And yet some Lesbians criticize us for living in woman-only space, for providing woman-only space for vacationing Lesbians, and for supporting other woman-only spaces. "How can you isolate yourselves, cut yourselves off from half the human race!" We assume the question is rhetorical.

SHE'S JEWISH, YOU KNOW! *December, 1987*

Irene and I were having a delightful conversation with a woman we do not know well, but like a lot. She was telling us about her life since we'd last seen her several years ago. Her lover was wonderful, her well-paying job was wonderful, her house, her health, her dogs, her garden, her financial state, everything was wonderful. We were laughing and joking and feeling great listening to Karen wax eloquent about her sweetie's good influence during their five years together. Then she said, "I've learned so much about managing my money from Jane. She's Jewish, you know." Silence fell. Looking surprised, Karen added, "No offense intended," and smiled. Because I like Karen, I took a rational approach. "That's a ridiculous statement," I said. "You know plenty of women who are good at managing money who are not Jewish." She nodded, still smiling. "Furthermore, you know plenty of Jewish women who are terrible at managing money." She continued to smile and nod. "That's right," she agreed. "Jane has two sisters and they hardly know a dime from a dollar. They are always broke." We'd barely begun to relax when she threw in her punch line. "Of course, I am sure they were adopted," she said, and she did not laugh. "I know what I know." She was not interested in further conversation and neither were we.

One evening, sometime before this happened, a Lesbian who had been friends with Irene for twenty years used our visit, the first in a couple of years, as the excuse to start drinking again. "Just some champagne in honor of the occasion!" she said. She was maudlin drunk in no time. She began re-telling the important moments in her friendship with Irene, including the times Irene helped her continue her education, pay her bills, find and keep jobs after her numerous alcohol crises. Before long she was attacking Irene, calling her "stingy," "exploitive," "money-grubbing," and other money-related epithets. She prefaced her remarks with phrases like, "it's not because you're Jewish, but." Nothing Lynnette's lover or I did or said could stop her. The Jew-hating diatribe that spewed from her mouth shocked all of us. Irene refused to leave, "until I hear it all." Then we left, never to see or talk to her again. "She hates me," Irene responds when we return yet another letter of apology. "She would vote for Hitler."

Less than a week later, we were having an RV conversation with a woman and man in the parking lot of Camper World when the man said he'd gotten a good deal on his RV because he'd "jewed down" the previous owner. We angrily confronted him with his anti-Semitism. The man was genuinely astonished. He had never connected the phrase with Jewish people. He apologized, thanked us for the lesson, and swore he'd not use the term again. Irene now waits uneasily for its recurrence in our frequent conversations about the price of things with friends and strangers.

There is a long and dishonorable history behind the myriad Jew-hating slurs, stereotypes and crimes relating to money. It started early in the Christian era when the church decided that usury, charging interest on money loaned, was unChristian and a grievous sin. Well, as it turned out, the Christian imperative to help one's neighbor seemed to break down when it came to lending money without charge. These saintly folk were in a dilemma. They solved it by assigning the function of money-lending to the unChristian "sinners" in their midst, the Jews. A few of these Jewish "bankers" and "finance companies" became rich, but most were just conduits through which capital changed hands during those centuries preceding the rise of the capitalist economic system in the modern era. This meant that for more than a thousand years Christians, from a peasant needing a few pennies for seed, to Isabel and Ferdinand seeking the money for Columbus' voyage, had to borrow from a Jewish money-lender. They had to ask for money, promise to repay, make excuses when they didn't repay, forfeit the collateral, pay the money back and pay interest to someone who was unchristian enough to lend money for a fee in the first place.

The situation was exacerbated by several other factors. Throughout most of their history since the Christian era began, Jews have been forbidden to own land, to live where they choose, to seek ordinary employment, to mingle with Christians. They were the "outsiders," hated and scorned as "Christ-killers," the subject of superstition and tales. At certain times in certain places, they did achieve citizenship, acceptance and a semblance of integration, at least in the upper classes, as in Spain before their expulsion in 1492 and in Germany before their massacre by the Nazis. But usually Jewish people have been forced to live huddled together for protection in separate areas of villages, towns and cities. The guilds, the universities, the professions, the army, the church, and any level of "government" service were closed to them. Denied employment by Christians, except as money-lenders, they became shopkeepers, peddlers, import-exporters, and the employers of other Jews. Their only personal interactions with Christians involved the buying and selling of goods and services. All this made it easy to get a gang of boys, or a village or a regiment, to plunder, rape, murder and destroy the bodies and possessions of such a "strange" group of people -- especially when money was owing them. All of this made it easy for us to think of money when thinking of Jews.

It is unlikely that Karen knows anything about the history of her belief about Jews. She believes it in spite of the living evidence to the contrary embodied in her lover's sisters. This ability to ignore the mass of "evidence to the contrary" is what makes cultural, racial, sexual stereotyping so dangerous. For a millenium, Christians have been able to ignore the poverty of most Jews, because, like Karen, they believe Jews are good at managing money. And like Karen, they think up something, anything, to keep the belief intact. There is no way to know how many Jews have been murdered by thugs and soldiers and "good Christian" neighbors who were sure they had money hidden away.

The anti-Semitic person perceives the behavior of Jews as being different from that of non-Jews. For example, the ability to bargain, to get the best price for something when buying or selling, to get the most for one's money, not to be cheated, not to be "taken" is one we all wish we had, one

82

which we admire in others -- unless that "other" is a Jew. Also Lynnette may have harbored resentment towards anyone who helped her, but she wouldn't think that person a money-grubber for expecting her to repay the money she borrowed if her benefactor had been a Christian. And she might have remembered she was never charged interest, if Irene had not been Jewish.

Anti-Semitic perception distorts more than money issues. Jews are called "clannish" because laws, violence and the fear of violence, discriminatory real estate practices and the need to live among friends in a hostile environment cause many Jews to live in "Jewish neighborhoods." The same negative judgment is made because Jewish employers tend to hire other Jews. Different reasons are given for the existence of other ethnic, racial and religious neighborhoods, and for the hiring practices of their inhabitants. The fact that white Anglo-Saxon Protestants tend to live in their own neighborhoods goes unnoticed of course, as do their tendency to hire their own.

It is impossible to do more than bring up the subject of anti-Semitism in a short article. I was impelled to bring it up now because Irene and I had just gotten comfortably into reading aloud a biography of Willa Cather, really loving the book, when the author brought up the subject of Cather's virulent anti-Semitism. We were so upset by the examples she gave that we had to put the book away. There is nothing I can do to raise the consciousness of my departed Lesbian sister,

Willa Cather, but perhaps this piece will keep another Lesbian sister from hurting my companion lover. She's Jewish, you know!

Non-Jewish readers interested in learning what some Jewish Lesbians think about their Jewishness and Lesbianism and about their oppression as both will find *Nice Jewish Girls* edited by Evelyn Torton Beck, and *My Jewish Face & Other Stories*, Melanie Kaye/Kantrowitz, both published by Spinsters/Aunt Lute Book Company, San Francisco, valuable and fascinating books. Buy them for yourself for Christmas.

THE SUMMER OF '73   *July, 1985*

The summer of 1973 was momentous for two Los Angeles Lesbians I know. Rosalie and Jean, who had known each other since the sixth grade, were best friends. At sixteen, they were "making out" behind the stacks at the library. When they graduated from high school, the summer of '73 and all the seasons to come stretched before them, empty of the daily companionship and the sessions behind the stacks they craved. Like so many other young Lesbians, they had little unaccountable time and no privacy. They were desperate. Their friend, Pam, arranged for them to consult with a counselor/minister at the Metropolitan Community Church, who affirmed their right to live Lesbian lives independent of their families.

Emboldened by this recognition of their adult status, they decided to spend the night together. After phoning appropriate stories to the appropriate people in their families, they checked into Room 212 of the Riviera Motel at Sunset and Highland in Hollywood and had a glorious time.

Their "together all night in a bed" experience intensified their desire to live together and gave them the courage to make the next move, that of sharing their plans with their families. Jean lived with her sister and knew she'd have little trouble from her. However, they feared that Rosalie's mother, possessive and protective of her precious daughter, would have a fit. Still, they thought, she does really love Rosalie and wants her to be happy. Perhaps, faced with the ecstatic joy apparent in her child, she might even be pleased by their transformed relationship. They decided to give her the opportunity to be pleased.

The young lovers, accompanied by their friend for moral support, used the long bus ride from Hollywood to the suburbs to re-invent Rosalie's mother, endowing her with all the understanding and empathy they needed. Alas, it was the real mother who greeted them and heard Rosalie's declaration of love and her "happily ever after" plans. Reverting to her more expressive Italian, Rosalie's mother let it be known to Rosalie, Jean and their hapless friend -- and the rest of the family, and the neighbors, and the Virgin Mary and all the saints -- what she thought about her darling daughter doing unspeakable things with anybody, especially her girlfriend, making unthinkable living-together plans with anybody, especially her girlfriend, and asserting unholy love for anybody, especially her girlfriend. The commotion brought the father in from the backyard and caused him to evict Jean and Pam from the house minus their purses and other belongings. Stranded penniless in a strange neighborhood, terrified by the scene they'd just experienced, and apprehensive about Rosalie's fate, Jean and Pam made their way a mile or so to a gasoline service station where a sympathetic attendant allowed them to use the phone. They called the MCC minister, who drove over and got them, calmed them with reassurances and took them home.

Meanwhile, Rosalie was held prisoner by her family. She was never left alone. Her mother slept on a sofa pulled across the front door at night. Poor Mother, railing against Jean and heaven and fate for bringing such trouble to herself and her family. The priest was no help either. He told her to calm down and leave her daughter in god's hands, that love was a gift, not a curse. For many weeks, Rosalie responded with Lesbian pride and with the familiar "I have the right to live my own life" refrain, invoked unsuccessfully by unnumbered generations of young people. When this honest expression of her feelings had no positive effect upon her mother, she lied with success. She told her mother she was sorry for causing all this trouble, promised to forget Jean and their plans, and offered to bake a gingerbread cake, her father's favorite, to demonstrate her repentance. Her mother, wanting to believe, thanked the Virgin and let Rosalie go to the grocery store for ingredients. And, just like in the movies, our escaped heroine was soon reunited with her lover, and they lived more or less happily ever after, companion lovers for twelve years, and loving companions to this day.

I recount this true Lesbian story, not because it is unique, but because it is not. Just about every Lesbian can find an echo of one of our own Lesbian life stories in this story of Jean and Rosalie. My mother still prays for my heterosexual conversion; and when my companion lover was a young Lesbian, her mother tried to imprison her at home. Most Lifelong Lesbians remember their favorite private place, their own "behind the stacks at the library." We recall violent scenes with our own or our lovers' parents, siblings, husbands, children. Our struggles to lead happy Lesbian lives is what Lesbians have in common with each other. It is this common struggle, and the stories our lives produce as a result of that struggle, that allows us to identify with each other, to experience a connection with each other even though we may live very different lives.

Take Rosalie and Jean for example. The library they used for their private place is at the Foundation For the Junior Blind in Los Angeles. Jean is blind; and Rosalie, though "legally blind," is partially sighted. Their disabilities give them a somewhat different perspective and social reality than that of sighted Lesbians, and add "vision" details to their Lesbian stories. For instance, Jean and

Pam, who are blind too, walked that mile or so from Rosalie's house without the canes they needed to locate obstacles and curbs. They could not see street signs nor could they look around for a place to phone. However, they were very much the same as any other Lesbian in their experience of Lesbian life, and they remain *bona fide* members of the Lesbian community.

Sighted Lesbians, unfortunately, often treat visually disabled Lesbians as if they were their disability, rather than as Lesbians who are disabled in one way or another. This is the common complaint of disabled Lesbians about Lesbians whose physical disabilities are minor and/or acceptable and/or just haven't occurred yet. "Temporarily able-bodied" is the term used to describe the latter. Jean and Rosalie have some suggestions for behavior to help sighted Lesbians get along better and feel more at ease with visually disabled Lesbians:

1. Do not use the term "blind" as a metaphor for stupid, ignorant, evil etc. "How could she be so blind as to prefer Mary to me?" This word usage is insulting. It also encourages the notion that visually disabled persons *are* stupid.

2. When a visually impaired Lesbian asks for directions, to the bathroom for example, be specific.

3. When offering to assist a visually impaired Lesbian to find the bathroom (and it is perfectly correct to do so), say, "Would you like to take my arm?' If she agrees, gently bump her RIGHT el-

bow with your LEFT one and allow her to hold your arm. Never grab her arm and drag!

4. Never try to assist a visually impaired Lesbian by taking her LEFT arm. The left arm is the guide dog arm, her lifeline. So, even if *she* hasn't a dog, the next blind Lesbian you meet may.

5. NEVER pet a guide dog. NEVER! Or offer it food! Or play with it! NEVER! A guide dog is a *working* dog, not a pet.

6. Do not move the belongings or the chair of a visually impaired Lesbian without telling her SPECIFICALLY where they are.

7. Don't be embarrassed about noticing that the Lesbian sitting next to you cannot see what the sighted women are laughing about. Offer to describe the action.

All of the above will help us find new friends, new lovers too. I think Jean (or is it Rosalie?!) is single at the moment.

WE ARE FAMILY   *August, 1983*

Lesbians, as an oppressed minority, are significantly different from members of other oppressed groups. A major difference is our estrangement from members of other oppressed groups to which we belong: women, Jews, People of Color, disabled people, working and poverty class people. This estrangement frequently includes our family, religious group, childhood friends, neighbors, co-workers, colleagues. Lesbians (and Gaymen) are the only oppressed group whose "difference," if known, results in our separation from the very persons and institutions which assist and encourage other oppressed people to continue the struggle for liberation. It is a measure of our personal power, strength, determination and our love of women, that so many of us persist in living Lesbian lives despite the forces opposing us.

The Women's Liberation Movement gave Lesbians the opportunity to lessen our historic estrangement from women who are not Lesbians. Many Lesbians and Non-Lesbian women understood the connection between Lesbian freedom and the liberation of all women. They realized that women's rights to the control of their own bodies must include the right to choose women for sexual/affectional partners, or else their rights to abortion, to child custody, to freedom from sexual and marital violence and harassment would always be in jeopardy, would be conditional. However, there were other Lesbian and non-Lesbian feminists who tried to get Lesbians to behave as if sexual preference was of little consequence. They believed oppression as women was sisterhood enough, and wanted Lesbians to suffer exclusion, the trivialization and omission of Lesbian issues, personal insults and other personal and organizational manifestations of homophobia, without a fuss. As a reward for Lesbian "good behavior," feminist events would include a Lesbian something -- a workshop on "alternative lifestyles," a Lesbian speaker on a non-Lesbian topic, a C-R experience about Lesbianism for non-Lesbians. Lesbian issues were not considered feminist issues. Lesbian issues were "divisive," what Betty Freidan called the "Lavender Herring."

These obstacles did not stop Lesbians. Lesbians were persuasive, argumentative, blatant, rowdy and *insistent* that ALL feminists recognize Lesbianism and Lesbian rights as feminist issues, in their organizations and in the outside world. As a result of the continuing work of militant Lesbians, Lesbians and our issues are an integral part of feminist organizations, political theory and action. Lesbians made a home place within the feminist community.

In addition, Lesbian feminists created another homeplace, a visible Lesbian community of organizations, of artistic, educational, spiritual and social events, of books, newspapers, films, of professionals and artisans. We have, in fact, recreated, in our Lesbian community, the persons and institutions we need to assist and encourage us to continue the struggle for our liberation.

WELL, ALMOST!

Lesbians of Color tell white Lesbians that they don't feel "at home" or assisted and encouraged in much of the Lesbian community, that most of the Lesbian community is white and racist. White Lesbians are saddened, shocked, annoyed, surprised, dismayed, and/or furious at the telling. Haven't we said, announced, created outreach committees, issued directives, passed resolutions, published letters to let Lesbians of Color know they are welcome at "our" organizations, projects, political actions, retreats and socials? Haven't we even appointed some Lesbians of Color to our steering committees and boards? It isn't our fault, we say, that Lesbians of Color do not respond to our efforts, except to criticize anew. We cannot be blamed if Lesbians of Color *divisively* insist that racism is a Lesbian issue and expect white Lesbians to eliminate the personal and institutional racism which keep them marginal in the Lesbian community. Isn't our shared Lesbian oppression more important. . .?

Familiar, isn't it? It is disconcerting, to say the least, to see and hear white Lesbians respond to criticism and demands from Lesbians of Color with words and behavior like those of non-Lesbian feminists (and Gaymen in Gay organizations) when faced with Lesbian militancy. White Lesbians need to remember the anger and frustration we felt at those experiences, so we can hear our Sisters of Color with attitudes we wanted from non-Lesbian feminists. If we do this, we may be able to initiate and/or welcome necessary changes in a true sisterly fashion. Indeed, we are sisters, members of a family separated at birth by circumstances over which we had no control. We are grown-ups now, and together we can control our circumstances enough to create a Lesbian community which will be home for all of us.

MEMORIES FROM THE GOOD OLD DAYS
Feminist Women's Health Movement *Sept., 1989*

In 1972, while Ronald Reagan was governor of California, the Los Angeles Police Department, the American Medical Association, and the Attorney General's office were giving the Feminist Women's Health Movement pioneers lots of trouble. They were particularly upset by the Movement's "self-help" groups and workshops. Indeed, the whole self-help concept upset them.

The first time I heard Lorraine Rothmann and Carol Downer speak, I was a little upset myself. Of all the interesting and new-to-me ideas they were telling us about, one was too much, off the wall, bizarre! for this married woman. They said that women who engage in sexual intercourse with men were umpteen times more likely to develop an assortment of syndromes, conditions, infections, diseases, including certain kinds of cancer, than women who do not. I believed everything else they said, but dismissed their sex with men concerns as proof that Lesbians don't miss an opportunity to chide non-Lesbians for the errors of their ways. A short time later, I became friends with Lorraine and was astonished to realize that she, and most of the other "man-hating Lesbians" she associated with, were not Lesbians at all.

Feminist Women's Health self-help groups and workshops were consciousness-raising with a difference. Women sat in a circle and talked about their lives, but the emphasis was on their bodies, what they didn't know about them and why, about their experiences with doctors and hospitals. Doctors were still secure on their thrones then, and most of us were shocked by what we were learning. We talked about pregnancy, childbirth, miscarriage and abortion. We talked about "tipped" uteruses, birth control, Lesbian health. We talked about sex. We realized that Lesbians and medical women were just about the only women who had ever seen the genitalia of adult females. Almost none of us had looked at our own. Furthermore, most of us didn't know we were missing anything by never having seen our cervix or our clitoris. We were still feeling grateful we knew we *had* a clitoris-- those of us who did know, anyway!

This is where self-help groups demonstrated their difference from C-R groups. The Feminist Women's Health Movement activists taught "self-examination." They got up on a table and showed us what our "private parts" looked like by showing us theirs. They taught us how to see our own in a mirror. They talked menstruating women, pregnant women, childless women, and old women into getting up on a table so we could see the differences in the cervix and vagina during such conditions. They showed us pregnancy changes and early indications of yeast infections. They gave us plastic speculums and showed us how to use them, and we did. We saw our cervix and the walls of our vagina, parts that doctors

talked to us about, parts they saw, but we didn't --
even though we could. They suggested we watch
ourselves masturbate (at home, of course), so we
could see what our own engorged tissue and erect
clitoris looked like, what sexual excitation looked
like. Those of us too shy or prudish to attend self-
help groups learned from our friends.

What a time that was! Before the Feminist
Women's Health movement, most of us still believed in our doctors, even though we no longer
believed in other gods. Most of us didn't talk
about sex, except in whispers to our doctors. As
for masturbation, those who did it felt guilty and
didn't talk about it, and the rest of us had little, if
anything to say. We were astonished to realize
the extent to which we had allowed men -- doctors, husbands, lovers, sex "experts," therapists --
define our bodies for us. We were wild with the
discovery of the extent to which our bodies did
not belong to us. The Feminist Women's Health
Movement, through the self-help groups in
homes and at their Centers, helped bring about
the enormous leap of consciousness which resulted in women's more assertive attitude about
women's rights over their bodies.

That "Hundredth Monkey" leap was still ahead
of us during the time I'm writing about. The
Feminist Women's Health Center had just
opened in one of the huge old houses on
Crenshaw Boulevard near Olympic, in Los
Angeles, and the women were experimenting
with a new "self-help" technique. It was called
"menstrual extraction." It's purpose was to enable

a woman to extract all the blood, etc., of her period from her uterus at one time by the use of a flexible plastic tube of some sort inserted by the woman (with or without the help of a friend) into her cervix. I think it was Lorraine and Ellen who came to the steering committee meeting of the Orange County Center for Women's Liberation to tell us about it and to ask if some of us would come to their Center when our period was due so they could practice on us. Most of the women did participate, but Oh!, My! Not me!

Was "menstrual extraction" a euphemism, a camouflage for abortion? The FWHM women said it wasn't, said it was simply a way for women to have more control over our bodies. With this technique, we could eliminate the hassle and inconvenience of a three to seven day menstrual period. If a woman's period was late, if the fertilized egg was in the uterus, well. . . I was never very clear about that, and neither were they.

The LAPD wasn't clear about that either. They kept sending undercover policewomen to self-help groups. Then one night, late, after the groups had disbanded and almost everyone was gone, hordes of policemen invaded the Center. They waved their search warrant and began tearing the place apart. They said they were looking for evidence of "practicing medicine without a license." They certainly were looking for the Center's mailing list and records. Those were kept in a soft leather satchel and carried home every night "just in case." One of the women, dressed in a full skirt, picked up the satchel when

she heard the police, tossed it on a large, uphol-
stered chair and sat on it. She didn't move for
hours as the police turned over drawers and
rooted through papers looking for names.
Giving up finally, they arrested Carol Downer and
another woman, whose name I am sorry to have
forgotten[5], and left.

I received a call about midnight and, petrified,
drove into Los Angeles to join the other women
at the Center. Dozens of us were making phone
calls, addressing envelopes, and cranking out letters on the mimeograph machine. When the post
office opened in the morning, we had hundreds
of letters ready to mail to feminist groups and individuals, giving information and requesting
money and specific kinds of assistance. Demonstrations and rallies came next. On the day of the
trial, hundreds marched in front of the
courthouse, overflow from the packed courtroom.
The December, 1972 issue of **OFF OUR BACKS**
reported:

UPPER FOR DOWNER

Carol Downer, co-director of the FEMINIST
WOMEN'S HEALTH CENTER, was acquitted of charges
of "practicing medicine without a license." She was arrested after having helped a friend diagnose a yeast infec-
tion and insert yoghurt as treatment. The law defines
practicing medicine as diagnosing and treating a disease.
Downer's defense attorney, Diane Wayne, said the statute
was so vague that "she wouldn't be able to discuss a cold
with a friend or offer her a Kleenex for it," and "half the
mothers in the country could be charged with diagnosing
that their children had measles."

Downer's acquittal set a precedent which enabled self-help clinics to continue their work. Nothing "official" was said about menstrual extraction. Feminists celebrated this victory, though I must confess some of us wished we could have used one of the strategies we thought up that hectic night at the Center. If the courts had decided that women did not have the right to extract menstrual blood from their own bodies, we planned to call on all the menstruating women in America to send their bloody tampons and napkins to Ronald Reagan at the Governor's Mansion in Sacramento. I'd have loved to do that.

I've been thinking about this proposed action again, since the latest inroads in women's rights to choose abortion. If they are going to decide that a fertilized egg is a human being (that is what "from the moment of conception" means), then perhaps all the menstruating women in America can send *their* menstrual blood to George Bush, or the Supreme Court, for a decent burial. Until medical science can pinpoint that "moment of conception," and can tell the difference between periods with or without fertilized eggs, "preborn/unborn human" beings are being denied the right to a dignified burial. We have no idea how many "unborns" get unceremoniously flushed down a toilet or thrown out on a tampon or a napkin. I no longer menstruate; nor do I engage in sexual intercourse with men. Still I'd thrill to be part of the action, organizing, wrapping bloody packages, paying the postage, and reliving the excitement of those good old, bad old days.

HOMOPHOBIA AND DEATH IN THE CLOSET
September, 1985

I knew of a Lesbian couple who were companion lovers for thirty-eight years when death separated them. Nancy had no family to speak of, but Betty Jean's large and near-by family treated Nancy as "another daughter" and "another sister." She was Aunt Nancy to Betty Jean's numerous nieces and nephews. Together the two financed college for a talented but impoverished niece. Together they attended all important family events: birthdays, graduations, weddings, holiday gatherings. They participated in the ordinary daily life of the family too, the phone calls, impromptu visits, dinners and the endless discussions of the relationships of family members to each other and to in-laws and outsiders. Both women felt fortunate to be so lovingly embedded in "normal" family life as it is lived in the USA. They never talked about their own personal life, their own personal disagreements, problems and joys, of course. "It's nobody's business but ours," they'd say. Still, like so many Lesbians, they assumed everyone in the family "really knew" their relationship was Lesbian.

Nancy and Betty Jean had wills drawn up years before, wills they up-dated every so often as their assets increased. Except for a few bequests of particular objects to others, they were each other's sole beneficiaries. This, as everything else about their personal life, was not talked about, was private. When Betty Jean died, her family assumed that her half of everything was going to them. They were outraged to learn she had left her possessions to Nancy, a stranger, an outsider, someone she wasn't related to either by blood or marriage. They ransacked the house, shunned Nancy at the funeral, and talked to an attorney about the will. The careful years of legal preparation protected Nancy financially, but nothing could save her from the pain of losing her "family" when she lost her lover.

Another Lesbian I knew lived alone in her lovely canyon home when she became seriously ill. Joanne had had almost no contact with her parents and siblings in the thirty-some years since she moved to southern California from a small town in the midwest. She had a large circle of friends, Lesbians and Gaymen she had known for years. They were her family, all the family she ever wanted. An ex-lover, then her dearest friend, coordinated her care during her last months of life. Friends took turns driving her to treatments, sat with her during the day and kept a nightwatch as well. They ran errands, kept her house, helped her get her affairs in order. Joanne spent hours going over her possessions in her mind, deciding which ring or art piece was right for which friend, which Lesbian or Gay organization was to get what percentage of her estate. An attorney friend drew up her will. She gave friends instructions about her cremation and memorial service. When the end was near, she had someone contact her blood relatives. To her surprise, they flew in and were confronted with her Lesbianism for the first time. They banished Joanne's family of choice from her deathbed, turned them away from the christian church door and from the cemetery, and broke her will by claiming undue influence over a dying woman. They are now self-righteously spending Lesbian money.

A friend of my sister died in a boating accident recently. Carmela was in her late twenties, worked for the telephone company, and was very active in the Lesbian feminist community. She didn't own much -- a good stereo system, a word processor, some furniture, mostly second hand, and a car, almost paid for. She had a modest savings account and just about every Lesbian and feminist book published and every record. She was not out to her parents, and at her death, they destroyed her precious books and records, and sold what they couldn't use of her things. The money from the sale and from her bank account went to the parish church in her home town, stipends for masses offered for the salvation of her soul.

Irene and I talked about making wills many times. Once, the morning before we left for an out-of-town conference, we each wrote a simple will on some lined stationary and left them on the dining room table, "just in case." We felt silly when we saw them on our return. Not long after, we heard that the bereaved but irate family of a Gayman acquaintance broke his handwritten will with no trouble at all. We promised each other to make real wills "soon." Of course, we didn't .

Trouble over money and property when someone dies is not a specifically Lesbian and Gayman problem. Neither is it only the province of the rich. Still, homophobia does create particular problems for Lesbians and Gaymen, in addition to the ones we share with the larger population. Obviously, the fact that our companion lover relationships are not legal creates the greatest difficulty. The legal mating of heterosexual couples is a sacrosanct relationship. No matter how much parents, siblings or children may hate one's marriage partner or disapprove of the relationship, the inheritance right of that partner is inviolate, even without a will. Our out-of-the-law relationships are quite another matter. If we want our companion lovers to inherit our estate, we do not have the (heterosexual) privilege to indulge in any superstition or squeamishness about death and wills. We cannot afford to be lazy or thoughtless either. A legal, loophole-free will is a Lesbian necessity, one more price we pay for our audacity, for our insistence upon living with and loving another woman. In addition, we need to name as executor, a friend who can assist our beloved companion to stand up for her inheritance rights, should that become necessary. We cannot give our families the opportunity to behave badly, no matter how sure we are that they "really know" and accept our Lesbianism and our partner. In other words, we must be Lesbian cautious to the end.

Lesbians need caution in matters concerning our death and our possessions because many of our families have learned to ignore, "forget," or shield themselves from the Lesbian foundation upon which our "friendships" are built. Their self-deceit is usually the result of collusion between our families and ourselves, an unspoken agreement that if we do not discuss our personal lives with them, they will treat us as if we did not have personal lives at all. This covert contract enables us to fit into a "normal" family niche, that of the sexless, unmarried daughter, sister, aunt who, for some reason (after all, she was pretty enough!) couldn't get, or couldn't keep, a husband, so she lives with another woman in similar circumstances. In this way, the family does not have to acknowledge and "do something" about our Lesbianism, and neither do we. When we die and try to leave our estate to our "friend," the agreement is broken; and our families are left to deal with our Lesbianism without our help. It is not surprising that they frequently deal with it badly.

I am convinced that we Lesbians and Gaymen would be much better off if we gave our families the opportunity to adjust to our lives while we are living them. Those family members who cannot adjust with love, can adjust with politeness. If they can do neither, we can create families of choice from among the large and varied communities of Lesbians and Gaymen. Certainly heterosexuals expect their families to adjust to their choices. Heterosexuals do not "respect" their families' feelings about their love choices when those feelings are racist, anti-Semitic, or classist, for example, the way we "respect" our families' homophobia. Heterosexuals marry persons of the "wrong" race, religion, nationality, class. They marry persons their families think are too old, too young, too stupid, too educated, too lazy, too ill for them. They would not attend a family gathering at which an "unacceptable" wife or husband was not welcome. They demand their families accept or, at the least, tolerate their choices. And most families do just that.

Lesbians and Gaymen should demand no less from our families than our heterosexual siblings do. "But I love her/him," is all the reason heterosexuals think necessary to justify their choices. Why should we need more? And just as the knowledge of their "wrong" love choices does not cause the premature death of their mothers and fathers, neither will the knowledge that our love choice is the "wrong" sex kill off our folks. Our families' homophobia is a social disease that can be cured by love, patience, education and the everyday sight of Lesbian and Gay parents and grandparents, aunts and uncles, sisters and brothers, children and grandchildren, nieces and nephews -- and their companion lovers -- living our lives and our deaths out of the closet.

However, even those of us who are completely open and honest with our families need legal wills. Before Irene and I finally met with an attorney, we thought making wills was simple. We are each other's heirs. We thought that was all there was to it. We were wrong. We had to name those who would inherit our estates if we didn't survive each other long enough to make new wills. Except for a bequest to my mother, we wanted our estate to benefit Lesbians.[6] So we discussed, disagreed, and finally decided on which Lesbian projects to fund after our death. It was a fascinating process, one we recommend to all Lesbians.

The difficult part of the will process came when our attorney suggested, as additional insurance, that we specifically exclude from inheriting our estates those blood relatives who might be seen by the court to have a legitimate claim to our estate. This meant that I had to list the names of my children and state that they were to receive nothing from my estate. A lifetime of books and films about unnatural and vindictive parents disinheriting their children poured out of my memory to unsettle my resolve. Even though I knew they knew I was planning to leave my estate to Lesbian projects and not to them, I was impelled to write each of them, reminding them that my will had nothing to do with my feelings for them. And that is mostly true. Still, leaving money to one's children is the traditional way to keep the money in the patriarchal family. It seems more womanly, more Lesbian to leave our goods, our treasures, to the Lesbian family which nurtures us, to the Lesbian sisterhood which strengthens us, to the Lesbians who follow us --our true beneficiaries. Irene and I think of ourselves as womanly Lesbians to the end. ..and after!

A DEATH IN THE FAMILY *January, 1988*
Irma Georgina Middup

My friend, Middy, died last week. I say it just like that. My friend, Middy, died last week. Just like that, she is gone from my life. Just like that! I won't see her any more, won't talk to her on the phone, won't get cards and letters from her in the mail. This is the reality of death. One day my friend is here; the next day she is gone. I may believe that she inhabits an astral plane of higher consciousness; or that she peacefully awaits reincarnation; or that she now rests in the arms of Jesus; or that she has achieved nirvana; or that she lives in a heaven of dancing girls and nectar; or that she ceased to exist with the death of her body. Whatever my belief, it does not change the everyday reality of Middy's death. I had a friend whom I loved, and now she is gone. I am left with this vacant Middy-space in my life.

I don't remember how Middy and I first met. I know we took to each other right away. We remarked on this often, how we felt as if we always knew each other, how we had this inexplicable psychic connection. She had already turned seventy by then, but since her mother had lived well into her eighties, I assumed Middy would too. I thought we would be friends for a long time, would have plenty of time, needn't worry when we put friendship things off. I was wrong.

These are my favorite Middy stories. She fell in love with the little girl who sat next to her in their third grade classroom and was a Lesbian from that moment on. When she was a young woman about to enter secretarial school, she wanted desperately to meet someone like herself. While she was sure others existed, she did not know where to look for them. So she dressed for her first class in the style she imagined would be worn by the woman/women she was seeking -- slacks, man-tailored shirt, v-neck, sleeveless sweater, Argylle socks and loafers. She arrived early and sat in the back near the door where she couldn't be missed. She was weak with apprehension as skirt-clad women arrived and began filling the room. Finally, finally, the door opened and in walked a young woman, small like Middy and dressed like her too. Middy had found the other Lesbians and her first long-term relationship as well.

Middy transformed herself from the only child of an impecunious widow into a cultured, educated, "blazer-dyke" kind of Lesbian. She was a world traveler, a fine arts and folk arts lover. She could tell you in which restaurants to find the best food for the money, no matter what city you were in. She was teaching at the University of California at Northridge when she retired. She said she loved both the teaching and the retirement. She was pleased with herself, with her choices, with her successes, with her life. I remember one afternoon on our patio when Middy, Irene and I were discussing a friend who was hesitating about getting involved with a woman she thought would probably break her heart. "What's the matter with these modern Lesbians?" Middy mused. "What happened to 'jump right in and no regrets'?" She and Irene spent the rest of the visit swapping stories about the "good old-bad old Lesbian days" when Lesbians lived for love and had no regrets! No regrets! That was Middy!

In her old age, Middy became a feminist, disconcerting her old friends and former lovers. Her friendship network expanded to include Lesbian feminists of all ages. She began working with an organization of "senior" Lesbians and Gaymen. Soon she was having "feminist fits" about the sexist ways of the men. Later she gave up on them and worked only with woman-only groups, although she never wavered in her love and enjoyment of the Gayman who was one of her intimates. She was a member of OWN, the Older Women's Network and a founding member of the collective which organized the historic West Coast Celebration and Conference for and by Old Lesbians in Los Angeles, April of 1987.

Middy was planning to spend some time with us this summer in the house we had rented on Oregon's coast. Instead, she wrote and said she could not come because she had cancer and was going to die very soon. The ex-Marine Corps oncologist she went to told her she had three to nine months to live. Well, he told her the truth, but left her with no hope. She had a very hard time living what life she had left under those circumstances. Would she have lived longer if she believed that was possible? Before her death sentence, she talked about joining us for a winter visit to our Lesbian residential community and resort on the beach in north Florida. She was intrigued by the place, and wanted to experience living in a Lesbian neighborhood. "I'll be dead, don't you understand, dead by then," she yelled at me when I urged her to make the plan anyway. Would she be here with us now if she had been given a more indeterminate sentence?

Although Middy had a hard time living the last months of her life, she had a peaceful and happy dying. She died in her own home, surrounded by her own things, and lovingly cared for by her friends. She spent her last few days going through her things, organizing those which were going to the June Mazer Collection--Lesbian archives and which to friends. Her friends kept her company throughout her dying day. A card from me arrived that morning, so she knew I was with her also. I was told she remarked often of how happy she felt, how unafraid. She left us at 7:40 PM on Monday, November 23, 1987.

A DEATH ANNOUNCEMENT *1984*

In 1976, Mary Glavin created the Passing Game for the consciousness-raising presentation on class issues when she was a member of the Califia

Community collective. Her favorite question of the exercise was, "Did you expect life to be easy?" Mary did not expect life to be easy, but like everyone else, she wanted an easy life. She could have been, almost was, Cinderella. Her scholarship to Mills College provided the golden ladder out of poverty, ignorance and no choices. She earned a Ph.D. in Comparative Literature and taught at the University of California, at Berkeley. She married an artist with money in the family and had two children, a girl and a boy. She had a circle of interesting friends. Mary Glavin had arrived on Easy Street.

When Mary fell in love with a woman, she and her companion lover and their seven children fled the country, living in Europe for several years. Mary was willing, if it was necessary, to pay for her Lesbian choice with the loss of a university career and middle-class respectability. She hadn't had them long enough to believe in them anyway. She refused to pay for that choice with the loss of her children though. ""I'm a ferocious mother bear when it comes to my kids," she said. "I'm on my hind legs, swinging and biting then. Nothing easy about me there. *No one takes my kids*." No one did take her children, but the recurring custody battles with her ex-husband and his family kept her always cautious and on the edge of poverty. The pay for a private high school teacher did not stretch as far as attorney fees, and the "concerned" father felt no obligation to pay child support for the children.

Mary never lived on Easy Street again. She had to worry about money always, and she hated that. Worrying about money did not fit the "hippie" image she presented to the world. Once she called to tell me she was in a neck brace, and in pain, from an automobile accident. She was also out of work and out of money. That afternoon, she told me, she was sitting on the ground in her garden, trying to dig for vegetables so she'd have food, when she thought of her university job and started laughing. "It was laugh at this cosmic joke or die of it," she said, knowing I'd understand.

Mary was the reluctant heroine of her life, forced by the gift/curse of consciousness to try to do the right thing, no matter how difficult. She always tried to have the time and the space for the friend who needed a sympathetic ear, a bed for the night (or the week), a thoughtful critique of a paper or an idea. She had the humility and the skill of a born teacher who realized she learned as she taught. Those qualities gave her the patience for the consciousness-raising work on sexism, racism, anti-Semitism and all the rest, necessary at Califia Community sessions, in her classroom, and in her life. Her wry sense of humor and her sharp tongue were a big help too. She wished, sometimes aloud, for a "genuine show of emotion, like hair pulling or a fist fight," when witnessing another one of those interminable discussions of differences by a group of women using feminist process.

So Mary smiled and laughed and loved her children, her lovers, her students and her friends.

She was proud of Melissa, who followed her mother to Mills College on a scholarship. She was proud of sixteen year old Josh. "He is a sensitive human being of the male sex," she stated, "a joy to know." She loved her life. For years she struggled to quit smoking, praised me for quitting first. When she called to tell me she had abdominal cancer she said, "Isn't it a bummer? After all those years of feeling guilty about smoking!"

Mary Glavin did not have an easy life. She did not have an easy death either. She was uneasy about leaving her children before they were adults. She suffered great pain. She did not, *did not*, want to die. After four operations and more than a year of chemotherapy, Mary did die. She died at home, surrounded by people who loved her, about one in the afternoon, on March 2, 1984. She was fifty-one years old. I am unreconciled to her death.

GROWING OLD UNGRACIOUSLY *May 1990*

I don't remember how old I was when people stopped telling me I was young, too young, to know, to understand, what was wrong, misguided, impractical, about my statement, attitude, feeling, behavior. "This is wrong," I would say, or "not fair," or "unjust." Then my mother, one of the nuns or priests, neighbor women, strangers on the bus or subway, whomever I was speaking to would smile with affection, derision or annoyance, but always with condescension, and say, "That's what you say *now*. When you grow up, you will know better, will change your mind." I HATED that.

Years later, I realized I must have "grown-up" because people with whom I'd get into discussions about issues would say things like, "Why don't you grow up and act (think, believe) your age!" Or they'd say,"You certainly haven't learned much with age." Now many of my Lesbian peers use different terminology to communicate a similar message. "You are still so judgmental (or negative, uncompromising, angry)."

Lately I've noticed an addition to the criticism above. I've realized that some folks think it's time I started mellowing, as in "mellowing with age." "When are you going to mellow?" I will be fifty-eight in June, so I am certainly on my way to being old, whatever old is. Am I mellowing? No, I am not. Do I want to? I don't think so. I don't know if I am capable of mellowness. Is mellowness a desirable state?

I read articles praising the courageous young people who tried unsuccessfully to bring democracy to China. I listen to the excitement about democracy movements in Eastern Europe and the Soviet Union. I am moved by the words and the concepts. And then I remember the demonstrations of young, and not so young, citizens of the USA in the sixties and seventies. Our demonstrators, our protesters, wanted an end to war and a redefinition of American democracy to include rights and justice for our disenfranchised majority (Add up all "minorities," including women and we are the majority!). Because of our patriotic, very American, political actions, we were killed, beaten, jailed, expelled from school, refused school loans, not hired for or fired from jobs, threatened, spied on, ridiculed, vilified. Then we were co-opted. Our democracy movements have yet to recover their previous strength.

I could take note of this historical development, remember without rancor, if our government and its spokespersons and the other persons who have the public power to report, describe and interpret, would at least *mention* the difference in the way democracy movements are treated. Anything less is erasing history, is manipulation of the American "masses," is hypocrisy. Knowing this, how can I mellow with age?

Perhaps I could get mellow if our continuing struggle for equal rights, justice and an end to oppression was supported by those who praise the democracy struggles elsewhere.

I don't need a long memory to have a problem with ageing graciously. A short memory will do. For example, a few weeks ago I was reading an article in the **NEW YORKER** about the situation in Lithuania. Irene's parents were from Lithuania, which added to my interest in the article. Without any stimuli I could recall, a little girl from Florida popped into my mind. Her father is rich. Her mother is an ordinary working woman, a nurse. They are divorced. Ashley, who is three, told her mother in her own child words how her father sodomized her with the participation of her step-mother and in the presence of a man who filmed the event. Before the custody hearing occurred, the mother's attorney was hospitalized for an emergency appendectomy and peritonitis. The judge refused to grant a continuation until the attorney was recovered. The mother asked Garnett Harrison and her equally impoverished male colleague, who are trying to change the way child rape (incest) is treated in the law, to be co-counselors with her ailing lawyer. She promised to raise $1,000 to pay their plane fare from Vermont. So three attorneys represented this sodomized girl child and her mother. Even with irrefutable physical evidence to substantiate the child's story, the hearing was a legal and a human farce. Its outcome is a tragedy. The judge gave Ashley into the sole custody of her rapist father. The mother was granted limited supervised visitation. In addition, the judge said he would not reconsider the ruling until and unless the mother submits to two years of psychiatric treatment. Who could be mellow, knowing this?

Garnett says it would cost thousands of dollars to appeal the judge's decision. What does it mean to live in a democracy when a three year old child can't find protection in our courts of law? What do the democracy movements in Rumania and Estonia mean to children raped by their fathers in those countries? If they knew what Ashley knows. . .?

I think this is not the time for Lesbians, feminists, women *of any age* to become mellow. We know better than anyone the limits of democracy in our country. We need to express our anger about our lack of rights and justice. Talk about mellowing is just another way to disempower us, to keep us quiet, to keep us grateful that things are not worse. But they are worse for Ashley. She needs us to remember that as long as she is not free, none of us are free.

Dorothy Sayers said "... an advanced old woman is uncontrollable by any earthly force." It is my ambition to achieve that state. I recommend it as an ambition to all women. Oh! What wonders we could work!

[5] The name of the other woman arrested with Carol Downer was Colleen Wilson.

[6] After all, if Lesbians do not financially support Lesbians and our projects, no one will. We think it unconscionable that Lesbians so often leave their money, by default or by design, to the very persons and institutions that are the causes, the instruments, or the beneficiaries of our oppression. They leave money to family members to whom they cannot speak the "L" word, to persons whose social and economic heterosexual privileges save them thousands of dollars in fees, premiums and taxes every year, to churches that teach homosexuality is a sin, to schools, colleges and youth groups which harass or condone the harassment of Lesbians and Gaymen. Even "good" causes like cancer research and the March of Dimes can get along without Lesbian money left to them by our sisters. Our Lesbian good causes cannot.

III Gatherings

INTERNATIONAL WOMEN'S YEAR
a Spot of History *–published in 1990*

I attended the International Women's Year Conference in Houston, Texas, November 18 - 21, 1977, as one of the ten out-Lesbian delegates from California. For weeks before the conference, the political and religious radical right threatened to disrupt the conference. The Ku Klux Klan promised violence. Let me tell you, we were scared! The disruptions and violence did not materialize in any organized way. However, the pickets and demonstrators were there, calling us names and being obnoxious. Also, it was dangerous to cross the street. Men in cars would see us ready to cross with the green light and speed to the corner, coming to a stop with a squeal of brakes, inches from us. They would grin, "Welcome to Houston, Ladies."

The most annoying disruption occurred spontaneously, with nothing more necessary to its success than the hatred of the "regular guys" for women in general, and feminists and Lesbians in particular. Many of the 2,000 delegates had reservations at the Hyatt Regency, including me. When we arrived, the lobby was packed with women, in lines or milling about. There was luggage everywhere. It was reminiscent of Los Angeles airport when it's fogged in. Rumors were rife. As it turned out, an organization of construction companies had just ended their conference in the Hyatt. When the members learned who was coming in after them, hundreds of the men refused to relinquish their rooms. They stayed in Houston another night for the sheer pleasure of causing trouble for the Lesbians and feminists. I do not know how they felt about the trouble they caused the hotel staff which had to find comparable hotel rooms elsewhere for all of us.

The California delegation was seated near a couple of Mormon-dominated state delegations. We saw Mormon women sobbing as they voted against government funding for shelters and programs to assist battered women and abused children. We saw others in tears as they voted their conscience, not the dictates of their Elders. We saw the chairperson of one delegation, I think it was Montana, grab the hair of one of her delegates and shake vigorously, yelling at her, threatening her, each time she refused to vote the Mormon/radical right agenda. I often wonder what happened to those recalcitrant Mormons, wonder if Sonia Johnson's actions inspired them to rebellion.

The highlight of the conference for many of us was the sight of an overwhelming majority of the 2,000 delegates standing up to vote "yes" for the civil and social rights of Lesbians and Gaymen, including custody and adoption rights. It was hopeful to see Rosalynn Carter, the wife of the president of the USA listed as the honorary chairperson of the conference, to hear her give a speech, to see her in attendance too. The conference ended with Margie Adams leading us in three-part harmony, singing "We Shall Go Forth From This Place." There wasn't a dry eye in the hall.

Thinking about IWY makes me feel like weeping. It is history, and like most other rebellious events in American history, it is being erased and/or distorted. I can't imagine another conference like it happening again, at least not any time soon, at least not in this country. I can't imagine the Messrs. Reagan, Bush or Quayle .... I can't even finish that sentence.

OLD IS IN *June, 1987*
The West Coast Celebration By and For Old Lesbians

At the opening session of the first Celebration and Conference by and for Old Lesbians on Friday night, April 24, 1987, Janny MacHarg, an old Lesbian from San Francisco, sang the song she wrote for the occasion. Titled "Old Is In" and sung in swing tempo, Janny's song epitomizes the spirit of this historic Lesbian event. Here are the opening stanzas:

If you were around in the forties
And you thought that you couldn't win
Take heart now--Take part now
'Cause Old is In.

If you hung around in the closet
And thought what you were was a sin
Don't pout now--Come out now
'Cause Old is In.

These sentiments were loudly cheered by the almost 200 Lesbians at the conference, 80% of whom were at least 60 years of age. For the first time in the lives of most participants, we were at a large Lesbian gathering where the predominant hair colors were gray and white. The women were wildly enthusiastic throughout the weekend, thrilled to see so many Lesbian peers. Old-time Lesbian performers, activists, personages, and lots of ordinary Lesbians (as if any Lesbian could be called "ordinary!") from the United States, Canada, Mexico and England talked and sang, talked and danced, talked and flirted, talked and performed, talked and went to workshops, talked and talked and talked. The conference was one of those unforgettable, high energy, sparking experiences Lesbians are so good at organizing.

"I'm exhausted from having sat on a cloud all weekend."
Gerry Faier

Party-time was not the only activity of the weekend however. This was a crowd who knew how to work, too. Before the closing ceremony on Sunday afternoon, an international association of Old Lesbians had been founded, and so had a support task force, Anti-Ageist Lesbians, for women under 60. Individual women volunteered to assertively encourage the Lesbian, feminist and Gay print media in their home areas to publish news items, announcements, short pieces, sent to the volunteer by both of these new organizations. Task force members made plans for putting together an anti-ageism consciousness-raising kit for use in small groups and for in-service workshops for Lesbian and Gay service providers, community organizers, and academia, including gerontology and women studies programs.

Some Lesbians who call themselves old,
  Were tired being left out in the cold.
  So we had a convention
  And it is now our intention
  To meet every year. We are so bold!
    --Vashte Doublex

For most participants, being in the company of all those wonderful women was the most important part of the conference. Running a close second for me was the experience of listening to Barbara Macdonald speak, formally at the opening presentation and informally in conversation. She is so SMART! And what a speaker! Her thoughts and ideas leave her mouth in words that are clearly and logically organized and whose meaning is accessible to her listeners regardless of their education. Her analysis and her examples of ageism and of the ways external and internalized ageism harms all of us can be a most liberating experience for her audience. Aging is a biological fact; but it is also an experience we fear because we carry the dread of the old woman within us. We imagine her, old and ugly and boring and not like us. We do not have to dread our arrival at each age plateau, Barbara tells us. She jogs our memory of dreading thirty, forty, fifty, and realizing what we dreaded was not there, of thinking that it must be still ahead of us. The dread is of nothing, she reminds us, because we are ourselves at every age, and will continue to be so. She reminds us that we Lesbians say "NO" to the adjustments expected of women at every stage of our lives; and old Lesbians are no different. The grandmother stereotype is as oppressive to old Lesbians as the wife/mother stereotype is to younger women. Those of us who struggle against the attempts of young Lesbians to turn us into the mothers they wish they had, can imagine with horror being turned into their grandmothers!

It is impossible for me to do justice to Barbara's ideas in one paragraph. She and her companion lover, Cynthia Rich, wrote *Look Me In The Eye*, a groundbreaking book on aging and ageism. Read it and be dazzled by their brilliance. But reading is not enough. I think that all Lesbians who want to look forward to being old Lesbians someday, and all Lesbians who want to see that the Lesbian community is a safe and welcoming place for old Lesbians, including ourselves, need to hire Barbara Macdonald to give talks at our events. She can bring new life and new ideas to any meeting or banquet or fund-raiser or any other Lesbian event.

TWO/FOUR/SIX/EIGHT! ARE YOU SURE YOUR GRANDMA'S STRAIGHT?

Some other highlights of the weekend were: singing "Happy Birthday" for Merle Markland's 85th, Kate Rosenblatt's 65th and Vashte Doublex's 60th; Pat Bond as "Beloved Hick" The Love Story of Eleanor Roosevelt and Lorena Hickok; being with Phyllis Lyon and Del Martin, founders of the Daughters of Bilitis, being in on the founding of another pioneer Lesbian organization; Kate Rosenblatt's one act play performed by the San Francisco Readers Theater; the art exhibit and the Old Lesbian banner decorating the hall which was coordinated by Muriel Fisher; my ageism C-R group; meeting some of the women featured in the films *The Word Is Out*, *Silent Pioneers*, *Before Stonewall*, and in the book, *Long Time Passing*; Shevy Healey leading us in her visualization of a non-oppressive society. Get her to do it for your group; it was WONDERFUL!

"Age is hard to place among my shifting feelings."
                    --Ruth Mountaingrove

On Friday night, after the opening program was over, those of us staying at the conference hotel took over its restaurant and talked for hours, breaking female stereotypes for the staff, while having a wonderful time. That was a highlight, too. And the Saturday night dance! Next time we will have more big band music!

"Age is a time of great wonder. Old is scary but exciting"

--Barbara Macdonald

However, the most important and change-producing experience of the Old Lesbian conference for me and for Irene, my 60 year old companion lover, was seeing with our own eyes the many different ways there are of being old Lesbians. One would think that we would know there are as many ways of being old Lesbians as there are ways of being young Lesbians and of being middle-aged Lesbians. It seems so obvious, now.

As of January, 1991, write for information to, Old Lesbians Organizing Committee (OLOC), Vera Martin, Coordinator, P.O. 14816, Chicago, IL 60614.

WASHINGTON WEEKEND *November,1987*

Our first unexpected pleasure in Washington, D.C. during the March On Washington weekend, October 9, 10, 11, 1987, was riding the Metro, the city's underground train system. The train was filled with Lesbians and Gaymen. I didn't have to nudge Irene and whisper, "What about her?" or "What do you think about him?" the way I usually do. It was obvious that we were surrounded by our sisters and brothers. We were in Gaytown, U.S.A. for the weekend, no doubt about it. Because Washington is such a small city, the presence of more than six hundred thousand visiting Lesbians and Gaymen was overwhelming. We filled the shops, the restaurants, the hotels, the museums and the streets. Everyone was talking about it. We were everywhere and we loved it!

On that beautiful, sunny Saturday afternoon, we attended the March's first official event, The Wedding: a demonstration for equal rights. The street in front of the Internal Revenue Service building was blocked off for the occasion. Thousands of us milled around, checking out the scene, greeting old friends and enjoying the fashion parade. Some Lesbian couples were dressed in matching tuxedos, some in matching "best women" dresses. One Lesbian couple went all out in bride and bride attire complete with veil and bouquet. A few Gaymen were dressed in groom and groom regalia, and some others wore suits with a discreet flower in the lapel. However, the great majority of the participants of The Wedding were dressed for a political demonstration in comfortable shoes and loose-fitting casual clothes.

Robin Tyler emceed The Wedding demonstration and she was in top form -- She looked positively scrumptious in her tux as well. She had the job of putting the event in its political context, and she did that with intelligence and with the energy and enthusiasm that makes her such a dynamic and personable speaker. She was cheered at the end of each sentence, and sometimes in the middle as well. Yea, Robin!

Several other speakers brought out specific ways Lesbians and Gaymen have our rights abridged and what legal remedies are available to us. Karen Thompson described her continuing legal struggle to be reunited with her disabled partner who was placed in the guardianship of hostile parents. She was an in-person example of what The Wedding demonstration was all about. Troy Perry gave a short keynote address that almost rivaled Robin's for rousing the crowd. He reminded us of our lack of freedom to be affectionate in public without harassment, the way non-Lesbians and non-Gaymen are free, by putting his arms around his lover and kissing him on the mouth -- right there on the platform in front of everybody! That was an electric moment.

Unfortunately, the "ceremony" part of the demonstration did not continue the high-spirited seriousness that preceded it. Instead it was uninspired, trite, and lackluster. And it was very, very long. It was nothing like the interesting, imaginative Lesbian commitment celebrations I've attended, and I was very disappointed. However, someone in my vicinity began passing out chalk when it became obvious that we were stuck there for a while. Instead of committing ourselves to "merging into one," we quietly and respectfully drew hundreds of chalk hearts on the street under our feet and wrote Irene & Marilyn, Brook & Pat, Bob & Fred, Sue & Jane; David & David and so on and so on and so on, in them.

That evening, we were seated in the Daughters of the American Revolution's Constitution Hall for the Lesbian and Gay Bands of America Festival Band with the Denver Women's Chorus and the Gay Men's Chorus of Washington, D.C. concert, "Let Freedom Ring." It was an artistic triumph and it was much, much more.

One of the concert's emcees was Pat Norman, Co-Chair of the National March on Washington. She reminded her audience that 50-some years ago Marian Anderson was not allowed to sing in Constitution Hall because she was Black. Then she said, "It is with great pride that I, a Black Lesbian, have the opportunity to emcee a program of Lesbian and Gay musicians. . . isn't it wonderful to be here and to be together!"

One special guest at the concert was Gerry E. Studds, the Gayman who represented the 10th district of Massachusetts in the U.S. Congress. He talked for a few minutes about his closet concern during the first Lesbian and Gay March on Washington in 1979. It was grand to see him on stage.

Then there was Nan Barrett. She is the conductor and artistic director of New York's Lesbian and Gay Big Apple Corps. What a beautiful woman! She conducted *Variations on "America,"* one of the show stoppers of the evening. The Denver Women's Chorus brought the house to its feet with its rendition of Margie Adam's *We Shall Go Forth,* and so did the entire ensemble performing *America the Beautiful.* Those of us who know that the lyrics of the latter

127

were written by a Lesbian, Katherine Bates, were particularly moved. The concert was a Lesbian and Gayman peak experience.

And then there was the March! We arrived early, so we could watch everything and everyone, including the *Rally To Assemble For the March* which took place from 9 AM till 1 PM, sponsored by the People of Color Caucus. We walked on the grass of the Ellipse staring and talking and listening for hours before we were told to get in place with our state or delegation or group. The milling around was such fun! It was like being at a gigantic party where it was OK not to know the other participants. It was fun to see people you had just seen last week and feel that rush of pleasure that comes from encountering the familiar in unfamiliar surroundings. Of course it was also fun to see old friends from other places and other times, and to watch others have those experiences, too. We saw most of the banners up close too. The Southern Witches of Atlanta, Georgia had an outstanding banner. Alaska's was gorgeous too. Lesbian and Gaymen's humor was rampant on others. For example: Preppy Faggots and Dykes, Lesbian Aunts, We're here because we're queer; Liz Taylor loves us; My mother knows/she doesn't like it/but she knows; Gay and Gifted; We were reminded of the seriousness of the occasion too with the many posters listing the names of men dead of AIDS.

The March took about five hours to complete. The first groups started off around noon. The rally at the Capitol, an hour's walk away, began around 1 PM. We marched with the banner of our friends from a Lesbian residential community in Florida. Our group hit the street at 3:20 PM. We were cheered on our way by thousands of earlier marchers. They were on the sidewalks, sitting on stairs, up in trees. They were indefatigable, still cheering and clapping and laughing hours after they'd begun. Perhaps being cheered by so many made up for the rally we had missed: Whoopi Goldberg, Jesse Jackson and all the rest. And we did get to do some cheering of our own. We yelled encouragement to the Lesbians and Gaymen of North and South Carolina, Delaware, Philadelphia, Pittsburgh and Washington, D.C., the only folks marching behind us. Yes, The Lesbian and Gay March On Washington weekend was a practically perfect experience for us. When is the next one?

THINKING ABOUT BOY CHILDREN
December, 1989

I've been thinking a lot about the issue of boy children since a really ugly incident erupted at the East Coast Lesbian Festival over the Labor Day weekend, 1989. The Festival brochure stated "girlcare" was available, a positive way of saying this is a female only event. Two Lesbians, co-mothers of an 18 month old boy, circumvented the organizers' intention by caring for their boy themselves and being discreet about his gender. Their subterfuge was uncovered, revealed to all in a most unpleasant way. The mothers awoke on the last morning of the Festival to find their cabin covered with signs: Pricklet Go Home; No Males In Lesbian Space; No Pricks Allowed.... Needless to say, the mothers were furious. They asked for support, and they got it.

A contingent of pro-boy Lesbians demanded mike time on the stage before the final concert at noon. The organizers, Lin Daniels and Myriam Fougere, demurred, citing lack of time for public discussion, voicing concern for the performers' feelings and their valuable equipment, in place on the stage. "We are going to read a statement from the stage," they announced. "You can have it peacefully, with no danger to the equipment; or we can storm the stage. It is your choice." Because of the threat, the organizers gave in. The statement, filled with generalizations about love and peace and "let's respect our diversity," was received with cheers and whistles and applause by most of the Lesbians present.

In the meantime, Myriam and Lin drafted Julia Penelope to make a pro Lesbian-only, women-only space statement. She spoke and was booed. She was hissed. She was yelled at. She was called names. "If it wasn't for your father, you wouldn't be here," screamed the Lesbian behind me, followed by roars of approval from others around us. Hundreds of furious Lesbians, their faces distorted by rage, shook their fists in the air. "You don't speak for me," they shouted, forgetting in their passion for the rights of boys and their mothers, that Julia belonged to the Lesbian diversity they were respecting moments before.

Most of the Festival goers were under forty years old. They haven't known a time without a visible Lesbian community. Most of them have not experienced their Lesbian life without the presence of Lesbian organizations and groups, newsletters, bookstores, books, records, concerts, festivals; doctors, therapists, psychics, chiropractors; Marches on Washington; Gay Pride Day, DESERT HEARTS and LIANNA in their consciousness, if not in their town. In fact, the Lesbians booing Julia Penelope, for reminding us how little Lesbian-only or women-only space there is on the planet and how much of what we did have is gone, haven't known a time when there was no turkey baster or physician-supervised "artificial" insemination for Lesbians at all.

As for Julia Penelope, she is one of those "Older Lesbians," those "before Stonewall" Lifelong Lesbians, the kind of Lesbian that younger Lesbians say they "need" as role models, that they "admire" for their courage. She is also the Lesbian who brought us one of the Lesbian community's most loved books, the original *Coming Out Stories*. She is one of the countless Lesbians who created the visible Lesbian community, wresting Lesbian space from the homophobia in the Women's Liberation Movement and the sexism in the Gay Liberation Movement. She did her share of demonstrating, organizing, confronting, teaching, writing, editing, speaking out for Lesbian rights, helping to make Lesbians visible to ourselves and to others. Yet she was booed from the stage by hundreds of Lesbians for trying to remind us how precious Lesbian space is, booed by Lesbians who have never really been without it.

It was a dreadful experience for me, one I have thought about and discussed often since it happened. I was stunned by the fury unleashed upon Julia. Why were so many Lesbians so passionately angry? I talked to some of them at the time. They said they were angry at the Lesbians who sneaked in the night and tacked the signs on the cabin. They hated the signs, too, said they were "hateful." They hated the way the mothers were treated. They seemed to see no incongruity between their delight in being at a festival that was bravely billed as a LESBIAN, rather than as a WOMEN's event and their rage at Julia for supporting the organizers' boy-free as well as man-free policy.

None of the Lesbians who defended the right of boys to attend a Lesbian event gave a thought to the right of girls to enjoy a few days free from the teasing, bullying, name-calling and ridicule that is common to boys in a group.

I thought about the two mothers who assumed they had the right to bring their boy to a Lesbian, male-free event. They are part of the growing numbers of Lesbians who are taking advantage of changing cultural attitudes, and are becoming mothers outside of licensed, state-supported sexual reproduction. They are the avant-garde in the world-wide movement toward the separation of the erotic from the reproductive in human life. They are the new Lesbian mothers, insisting they will raise a new generation of boys, non-sexist and caring about the rights of women.

Yet the attitude of these mothers toward their son was positively reactionary. They *could* use Lesbian-only, woman-only spaces as opportunities to teach their manchild that women have the right to limit male access to our spaces, our persons. Instead, they chose to allow hundreds of Lesbians to champion his right to erase a brief time of woman-only space for all of us. That is male privilege, alive and flourishing in the heart of a Lesbian feminist community, and this particular innocent baby has already experienced it. The experience will be intensified for him, and for all the other boy children like him, every time their mothers, and their many supporters, challenge woman-only space at events they attend, and every time they angrily absent themselves from woman-only events, complaining about "reverse sexism" and discrimination.

In trying to understand the why of such behavior, I found myself thinking of our female problems with boundary and access issues of all kinds. When I hear Lesbian mothers say they have been excluded from a woman-only space because their boy children cannot attend, I have to believe they are having trouble establishing boundaries between themselves and their children. They are fusing with the children, responding as if they and the children are one. The irony is that the

Lesbians who are supporting them also see them as fused, and are supporting that fusion.

This kind of Lesbian motherhood sounds to me like a minor variation of pre-Women's Liberation Movement oppressive motherhood, when mother was supposed to put her child and HIS interests first before all things that might be necessary, important, pleasurable for her. When children have, or "know" they should have, unlimited access to their mothers' time, space, resources, person, boy children learn that mothers/women exist to take care of them, while the girls, even those who grow up to be Lesbians, learn to be the caregivers of men.

I am beginning to think that the Lesbians who created this particular uproar in favor of male access to woman-only space, and the countless other feminists and Lesbians who did the same in the past, are acting out of their unconscious, internalized, female oppression, out of the training they received to be "women," that is to be mothers and wives of men, their caregivers, in the system of dominance and subordination we call the patriarchal family. Because of our training, we are unable to be "selfish." We can't put our interests and needs, and those of our oppressed sisters and the organizations dedicated to freeing us, ahead of the needs of men. We are still passionately committed to fulfilling the needs of men, whether they are our AIDS afflicted Gaymen brothers, our abusive, "misunderstood" fathers, or our blameless boy children at a Lesbian event. And we are ready to trash any Lesbian sister who tries to stop us.

P.S. Kay Hagan has written a small, brilliant pamphlet, "Codependency And The Myth Of Recovery; A feminist scrutiny," which bridges the space between feminist analysis of the family and twelve step programs approach to family. Write to her for a copy at 454 Seminole Avenue, NE #6, Atlanta, GA 30307.

IV. The Power of Naming

MANLESSNESS   *February, 1989*

The other morning, I was sitting across the table from Irene, reading a **NEW YORKER** magazine while she was working a crossword puzzle. We were drinking coffee and interrupting each other's activity with the ordinary conversation of our daily life. The sun was shining, the ocean breeze was warm and balmy, and the birds outside our door were having a chirping contest. We were enjoying ourselves, two more-or-less retired Lesbians in our pretty cottage in our Lesbian village, on a beach in Florida.

I turned the page to a review of a play, a play written by a woman and reviewed by a woman. The review begins, "At the emotional turning point of *The Heidi Chronicles*, Wendy Wassersteins' manless heroine Heidi Holland, an essayist and art-history professor, is supposed to deliver a speech at the Plaza Hotel." "Manless?" I started to droop. The review continued, telling about the speech and about the heroine's apparent sadness and then observes, "Moreover, the cause of Heidi's depression--her manlessness--is never alluded to." Heidi's manless-induced depression is not caused by a particular man's absence. She hasn't lost a lover or husband to death or boredom or another woman. She is a "New

136

Woman" so her manlessness is her milieu, her *gestalt*, almost her personhood. The reviewer, Mimi Kramer, sketches the plot and makes her comments. She likes the play and agrees with the author's point of view. The review ends with Heidi's "wish" for her adopted daughter, "that no man should make her feel she is worthless unless she demands to have it all." I almost wept.

On some days, it is more painful than on other days, to be confronted with the cultural lie that women need men in order to be happy. That day was one of the painful days. There I sat, a manlesss woman enjoying her life with another manless woman while reading shameless, blatant, untrue heterosexist propaganda that is soul-harmful to all women. Do Wasserstein and Kramer know Irene and I exist? What about our neighbors, women in my family, women friends and acquaintances, women we know of, all of whom are happily manless? Do they know about them? Do they know about the millions and millions of women in this country, Lesbian and non-Lesbian, who live with "manlessness," who, when their "manless" state comes to their attention, breathe a sigh of relief and gratitude?

The belief that the lives of manless women are incomplete, unsatisfying, unhappy, unimportant, depressed-- is one in the cluster of beliefs that is the infra-structure of women's oppression. It tells women and men that women must have a man of their own. No other ambition or achievement is as important, and without a man, ambition and achievement are futile. Since there is no reciprocal belief that women are as important to men's lives, men are under no pressure to direct their attention to the task of getting a woman of their own. They can go about their business, playing football, becoming educated, learning a trade, growing a beard, getting bald, even raping, beating, insulting and humiliating women, knowing that some woman will be "lucky" enough or desperate enough to "catch" him for her own.

Everyone, including men, knows that men aren't very nice to women, that "a good man, nowadays, is hard to find." I mean, how many Harvey Laceys are there? That's why women have to learn to be tolerant, to lower their standards, to forgive and forget. So he doesn't "help" with the housework or the kids. At least he doesn't run around on her. Well, Mary's man runs around, but he's a good provider. Jane's man doesn't make much, but he's a good father. Carol's man beats her, but she "can't help loving that man" of hers. Marilyn's man works hard and doesn't drink or physically abuse her, so she can't really complain about how tediously boring he is. And, when you come right down to it, a man of one's own, any man, is better for a woman than no man at all. I mean, what is a woman without a man? At the very least, a manless woman is DEPRESSED!

Is it any wonder that men are arrogant?

The function of a cultural myth is to erase from consciousness any facts that might contradict a basic belief upon which the society is based. The belief that women need men to be happy/fulfilled/real erases the unhappiness men cause women who live heterosexual lives. It erases the fact that almost all the women hospitalized for depression are married women with children. The belief erases the fact that women are more likely to be killed or abused by their own husbands and boyfriends than by the husbands and boyfriends of other women or by men who haven't their own women to kill or abuse. It keeps individual women from learning from their own experience and from the experience of other women. It keeps individual women trying to find, please and hang on to her own man.

The belief also erases from consciousness the existence of millions of happy single, divorced, and widowed women, those who are Lesbians and those who are not. We "know" about the desperate, discontented, man-crazy single women, divorced women and widowed women. Chris Cagney is the only cultural heroine I can recall who remained single because she loved her life the way it was. (Jessica Fletcher didn't remarry because her dead husband was so perfect no man could replace him.) As for us, the ordinary lives of ordinary Lesbians are invisible to almost everyone, including our families and co-workers. It is not in the "best interests" of men/patriarchy for women in general to know that there are lots of happy, fulfilled, manless women around. If all women knew about us, the work and suffering that accompanies finding, pleasing and keeping men might seem to them less a personal necessity and more an exercise of futility and masochism.

I know a Gayman who used to write screen plays for television sitcoms. He had lots of good ideas for Lesbian sit-com material. He was told again and again, forcefully, that Lesbians and Lesbianism are NEVER funny. The sight of ordinary Lesbians living their lives, enjoying themselves, or suffering from the same problems as "regular folks" isn't funny because it occurs without men. Golden Girls, Kate and Alli and all the other unmarried TV women are funny, but we are reminded frequently that they would *rather be married*, and that they know their lives are incomplete -- manless!

I'm not saying that "manless" women are, by definition, happy. We all have our troubles, some more disturbing than others. One Lesbian friend is depressed because she has lost her home, all her possessions, and her practice; and disbarment proceedings are in process in her home state. She is in contempt of court there for her efforts to protect her clients' children from their rapist fathers. Other friends are in varying degrees of sadness, emotional turmoil or depression because of illness, death in the family, intra-personal trauma, drug abuse or alcoholism, work or career problems, financial trouble, interpersonal problems with a lover, child, other family member or friend. My friend who just totalled her car isn't particularly happy right now either. Life is hard and full of problems which are unrelated to a woman's state of "manlessness."

Of course, we all experience varying degrees of happiness as well. Lots of the happy women I know bought houses recently and others are busy remodeling, painting, landscaping and doing all the other house-related activities we love. One recently learned she will perform at the Michigan Women's Music Festival this year. Others had poems, drawings, articles accepted for publication in '89. Some got new jobs, promotions, pay raises. Just about all of us have traveled this year. We went to plays, concerts, sporting events. We've had dinner parties, poker parties, pool parties. We've slept late, read novels, made love, cleaned house, shopped. Most of us, most of the time, are more-or-less happy with ourselves and our present lives, and look forward to a contented, woman-loving, woman-centered future. The myth about the results of manlessness is a bittersweet joke to us. We laugh at the ignorance of those who keep us invisible, but we mourn for the women our invisibility robs of the knowledge of a positive Lesbian choice.

AND THE WALLS CAME TUMBLING DOWN
July, 1987

Margaret Lewis died in May of 1987, just a week or so after attending the West Coast Celebration for and by Old Lesbians. She was 73 years old when a thrombosis suddenly felled her. Margaret was a small, wiry, muscular woman, cheerful and likeable. She hiked and climbed and worked and enjoyed herself to the very end of her life. She was a valued member of the San Diego Lesbian community and of the Sierra Club, both of which held memorial services for her. All of us who knew her will miss her presence in our world.

I was shocked by the news of Margaret's death. I knew her from the many feminist events we both attended in the past, but I hadn't seen her for a long time till we met again at the conference. We talked and remembered how fond of each other we were. Last time I saw her, she was moving tables and stacking chairs for the conference dance. I was unable to assist her because my right knee, injured in a roller skating mishap when I was 16, was in a particularly painful and disabling flare-up.

Because I was living through a disabled period while attending the Old Lesbian Conference, I was acutely aware of the cultural lie that says old age is, in itself, a disabling experience. My mother is 78 years old, lugs groceries and garbage and textbooks and art supplies up and down the stairs of her second-story apartment, and graduated from college with a Bachelor of Arts degree this spring. Until I attended the conference, I thought of her as an able-bodied exception to ordinary old women. She is not. What I am learning is that old Lesbians/old women, and even old men, live on a continuum of able-bodiedness even as you and I, and even as my children and grandchildren. I have the feeling that I used to know this truth once, that I am learning it again.

When I was having babies, I was very conscious of infant disabilities, infant diseases, and infant deaths. When I was the mother of small children, I was very conscious of childhood disabilities, diseases and deaths. The types and causes of adolescent disabilities, diseases and deaths were part of my everyday life when my children were in their teens. In fact, when I stop and think about it, diseases, physical and mental disabilities, and death have always been part of my everyday life. I have known babies born deaf, blind, with club feet, Down's Syndrome, muscular dystrophy, cystic fibrosis, cleft palate and cerebral palsy. I've known children who died of meningitis, leukemia, brain tumor, drowning and falls. I've known teenagers and adults who lived with, were temporarily or permanently disabled by, or died from multiple sclerosis, diabetes, tuberculosis, epilepsy, heart disease, myasthenia gravis, hepatitis, drug and alcohol abuse, war and sports and automobile and motorcycle injuries, mononucleosis, endometriosis, and Hodgkin's disease. Now I commiserate with friends my own age who are learning to live with middle-age diabetes, arthritis, high blood pressure, high cholesterol, menopausal discomfort; and I grieve for friends my own age who have recently died of heart disease and cancer.

Now that I am re-thinking what it means to be disabled, to be middle-aged, to be old, I wonder why I have always equated disease, disabilities and death with getting old, in spite of a lifetime of experience with death, disease and disabilities. I suppose the easy answer is that all people will eventually suffer some degree of degenerative disease/disability if they live long enough; and all old people die eventually, no matter how healthy, ablebodied or long-lived. Still, I wonder how come I did not integrate my experiential knowing that disease, disability and death are part of everyday life at every age with my knowing that it is part of old age? I am not sure about the answer to that. All I have are some tentative guesses at present.

I realize now that I constructed two imaginary compartments, "The Disabled" and "The Old." Into these compartments I have hidden from myself my fears of dying, physical suffering and pain, debilitating diseases, loss of sight and hearing, body integrity and attractiveness. They worked great for years. I was able to be a good friend to my friends who lost children and partners in death, to assist friends who became ill or disabled, to grieve over the "early" deaths of my father and my friends. As long as the walls of my compartments were intact, I never had to worry that disease, disability and death happened to ordinary, regular kinds of people, people like me.

In recent years, the Disabled compartment has sprung holes. First, deaf and blind women began attending programs I helped organize. They insisted we provide American Sign Language interpreters for women with impaired hearing. They wanted us to speak one at a time so the signers could interpret correctly, and so that each speaker could say her name before interrupting one another, so blind women could know who was speaking. They organized C-R and information-sharing groups so we could learn what was special about their needs and quit treating them like a "category." Of course they were right and, once I quit treating them as The F, I was able to like them or not like them only for the women they are. I also lost my terror of becoming blind or deaf myself.

Then I met a woman who has no control of any of her voluntary muscles except the ones in the first finger of her right hand. She is a politically active, Lesbian feminist writer and artist with whom I have lots in common in spite of the enormous differences in our physical mobility. Then two years ago, I was practically dragged to the disabled women's tent at the Michigan Women's Music Festival by two friends who insisted my "bad" knee, as I spoke of it, was a "disability" worthy of accommodations near the stage.

Now that "The Disabled" have names, have personalities, have coming out stories, have lives, have jobs, have families and lovers, and have become simply women with physical differences to me, my compartment for them disappeared. Its disappearance made it possible for me to accept my disabled knee and to seek treatment, something I was unable to do as long as I treated women with disabilities AS their disability. What a freeing process this has been for me!

As for "The Old," that compartment got a shaking when the women organizing the Old Lesbian conference decided to call themselves "Old," not older or some other euphemism, and decided that 60 years old was old! Then I went to the conference with my 60 year "old" companion lover and saw all those "old" Lesbians, many of them my good friends and my friendly acquaintances. Is this what "old" is? Is this what "old" looks like? Is this how "old" behaves? Then I met several sorrowful old women whose lovers were unable to attend the conference because they were dying of cancer or some other terminal illness; and I was unable to compartmentalize this information because of the recent deaths of my age-mate friends, June Mazer and Lee Woodward. Then I learned about Margaret's death and was shocked by the news. I was shocked anew to realize I thought of her death at 73 as an "early" one, just as I once thought my father's death of a thrombosis at 44 an "early" death. If Margaret wasn't old enough to die at 73, what age *did* I think was old enough? I didn't know, and my old/death link was strained to breaking.

My "Old" compartment is dissolving rapidly, though at present this is a mixed blessing. As my fear of being old recedes, I am beginning to experience fear of dying--but that is another story.

It occurs to me that we will not be able to accept and love our infirm selves, our disabled selves, or our old selves if we are denied or deny ourselves the opportunity to know and accept and love the infirm, disabled and old women who are part of our community. If our insensitivity to the special needs of some women keeps them from participation in our gatherings, all of us are the losers. This is a truth I am re-learning from experience and one I will not forget again.

MANHATING *September, 1982*

In the early 1970's, Gloria Steinem was a guest on a television interview program. At one point, the interviewer was trying to ask her a question, bumbling and stuttering and acting the fool. Finally Gloria rescued him by saying, "Are you trying to ask me if the Women's Liberation Movement is full of manhating Lesbians?" He admitted he had been looking for a tactful way to ask just that. Gloria responded by saying that many, many women in the Women's Liberation Movement were Lesbians because Lesbians, generally, are acutely aware of the oppression of women. She added that Lesbians are not usually manhaters, though. Women who live heterosexual lives, especially married women who really know what men are like, are the manhaters!

I was a manhating married woman when I saw that program and was pleased to hear my own observation about manhating expressed on TV by so astute a personage as Gloria Steinem. Lesbians I knew at the time were usually indifferent, if not outright bored, when the issue of men came up at meetings of the Women's Liberation Center of Orange County, California. Oh, they got into it when the subject was men as rapists, politicians, doctors, for example. But when the subject was men as almost half the human species, Lesbians would go to smoke, to pee, to sleep. Ho Hum!

147

So why does the population at large say "manhating Lesbian" as if the term were a hyphenated word? One reason given is that Lesbians must hate men if they prefer women as their lovers. One must question male logic here. After all, heterosexual men prefer women as lovers too; and no one calls them "manhating men!" In addition, these men who prefer women as companion lovers are the same men who rape, batter, abuse, humiliate, criticize, exploit, and ridicule women regularly. Even those "special" men we hear about are known to use the word *woman* as a pejorative: "You are different than other women" "quit acting like a woman" and "woman driver." They, in fact, are womanhaters; but since womanhating is normal in a patriarchy, no one is supposed to notice.

Womanhating (misogyny) has a long and dishonorable history. From the myths of Pandora/Eve bringing evil into the world, to the glorification of the rape of the Sabine women, to vagina dentata, to Freud's "woman as masochist," to Portnoy's mother, to the latest slut and old maid joke, to the man who is raping his daughter as I write this, mankind's expression of womanhating in thought, word and deed has been sanctioned by law and religion, through custom and literature, in the fine arts and popular entertainment. All this womanhating is hard to take when we stop to think about it, since each man had a mother who risked her life to produce him. Most men also had mothers who loved and nurtured them to the best of their ability. In addition, most men had/have sisters, daughters, aunts, grandmothers, sweethearts, lovers, wives, mistresses, and teachers, prostitutes, nurses, waitresses, aides, secretaries who smooth their lives, satisfy their needs and wants, and act as their magic mirror, showing them to themselves as better than they really are.

These male attitudes and behavior seem illogical to me. Womanhating men who prefer women as lovers call woman-loving women "manhaters." They declare shamelessly that women who prefer to live with and love women are unnatural, that women who refuse to live with and love men are unnatural, that women who hate men are unnatural, and that all three are the same: manhating Lesbians. Many indifferent-to-men Lesbians are taken in by this exercise in male logic. They get nervous and defensive when Lesbians like myself speak out to name man's crimes against women and to demand they stop committing them. These Lesbians call us "manhaters," as if there is something wrong with women, especially Lesbians, who hate men. I can understand their desire to separate our preference for women as companion lovers from our attitude toward men. But in our attempts to make that separation clear, we must not become the defenders of men, must not trivialize or ameliorate or erase their responsibility for the crimes they commit against women. We must remember that men expect women to forgive them their trespasses and to serve them with our approval--- *even when we do not sleep with them.*

MANHATING LESBIAN *October, 1982*

The subject of manhating makes most Lesbians nervous because people in the world at large link manhating with Lesbians, as in "manhating-Lesbian." This seems illogical to me since most Lesbians are not manhaters; and most manhaters are not Lesbians. However, putting the words *manhating* and *Lesbian* together makes a lot of sense if we look at the results of the coupling.

When a woman is known to be a Lesbian, those who know usually assume she became a Lesbian because she hates men. The Lesbian, herself, knows she is a Lesbian because she loves women; but she cannot get family and friends to believe her. In her attempt to be believed, she takes the only avenue open to her. She tries to show she does not hate men. She is nice to men; she praises men; she excuses and/or ignores men's womenhating behavior; she avoids criticizing men's behavior toward women. When a Lesbian is not out to family and friends, she is likely to behave in these non-sexual but man-pleasing ways in order to keep people from suspecting her Lesbianism.

The phrase *manhating Lesbian* has a similar effect on the behavior of women who are not Lesbians, since they also know the word linkage. This is particularly true of feminists who live heterosexual lives. They must be very careful of the ways they criticize the behavior of their lovers, husbands, male relatives, friends, colleagues, and men in general. Too angry or too general a criticism of men is likely to call forth the label "manhater," that is, "Lesbian."

Sometimes these man-pleasing tactics work and other people will be convinced that this "exceptional" Lesbian does not hate men, and this "exceptional" manhater is not a Lesbian. They will continue to believe that all other Lesbians are manhaters and all other manhaters are Lesbians because it is in the best interests of a patriarchal society to do so.

It is important to note the behavior which elicits the labels "manhater-Lesbian." At the top of the list is criticism of men's behavior toward women. It is customary to blame women for the bad behavior of men; their mothers taught them; a particular woman "drove them to it" or "allowed" it. When men rape their daughters, the mother is blamed for "not giving him what he needs" and not taking enough care of the girl. Girl victims of rapists and molesters are called "seductive." Women are blamed for our own sexual harassment, rape, battering. If we cannot bring ourselves to blame women for men's behavior we must agree with men that we are at least as much to blame as they are if we hope to avoid the manhater/Lesbian label. If we insist that men take responsibility for their bad behavior towards women and that they change that behavior, we are called manhater-Lesbian, no matter how we dress or with whom we live.

The second type of behavior that gets one labeled *manhater/Lesbian* is speaking out for the rights of women as human beings and citizens of a nation. Even if a woman uses her ingenuity and speaks of equal opportunity for promotions at work or equal access to professional careers *without* mentioning whose opportunities and access we want equality with, she is likely to be labeled, especially if she gets "strident" about it. If she dares suggest that the training and responsibilities of a nurse entitle her to a salary equal to that of a pharmacist (male) or a treetrimmer (male), and demands justice in the matter, she will definitely be called *manhating-Lesbian*.

Also labeled *manhater/Lesbian* is the woman who rejects a man's sexual advances in a way that does not leave him with the impression that she does so reluctantly because her husband or boyfriend wouldn't like it.

Then comes the "unfeminine" behavior rightly associated with Lesbians: rejection of marriage, preferring the company of women to that of men, "worldly ambition," non-apologetic athletic ability, intellectual excellence, making money, owning a business or a home, aspiring to or working at a "man's job," wearing tailored clothes and sensible shoes, owning a pick-up, a race car, a motorcycle.

Hence, the ways a woman can avoid the label *manhating Lesbian* are obvious: marry men and/or be sexually available to them and/or give the impression of availability, be uncritical of men's behavior toward women, be pleasing to men, defend and excuse men; be critical of women, take men's part against women; be satis-

152

fied with, or at least resigned to, women's roles, women's jobs, women's salaries, women's place in the world of men. We must behave the way men want women to behave and accept them uncritically. If we must complain, we must do so pleasantly. Every improvement in our lot or in men's behavior must be greeted with abject gratitude and remembered.

In this way the coupling of the words *manhater* and *Lesbian* is used to control the behavior of all women who want to change the way women are supposed to live in the world, both as individuals and as members of an oppressed majority.

It is time for women who live heterosexual lives to refuse to be intimidated by the Lesbian label. The implication that only Lesbians hate their oppression as women is insulting to non-Lesbian women. They need to correct that impression, and they need to do it while affirming their support of their Lesbian sisters.

As for Lesbians, it is time we stopped trying to prove we do not hate men. Instead, we need to demonstrate our love for women by participating in dismantling the man-made barriers to women's freedom which exist in the world and lurk in our minds. And one of those barriers is the fear that we will become the manhater everyone out there thinks we are. We need to give ourselves permission to recognize the truth when we see it, that men-in-the-flesh are the "people" who funded the Stop the ERA drive, who voted it down, who fund the anti-abortion and anti-Lesbian legislation, who use their power, position, and money to keep our wages low and to block our attempts to better our lives. It is men who pollute our environment, build nuclear bombs, wage war and profit from war, and sacrifice sons to war; who pay billions of dollars and earn billions of dollars on prostitution and pornography. It is men-in-the-flesh who make the world, the streets, the home unsafe for women and children and also for other men. If we think about this, it is possible that we may decide becoming a manhating-Lesbian is the most sensible, rational and caring kind of choice for a woman-loving woman. Believe me, Sisters, it is too soon to be a humanist!

TERRORISM IN AMERICA *August, 1989*

TERROR 1. Intense, overpowering fear. 2. A terrifying object or occurrence. 3. Violence committed by a group to attain a usually political goal.
TERRORISM The political use of terror and intimidation.
TERRORIZE 1. to fill with with terror; terrify. 2. To coerce by intimidation.
POLICE STATE A political unit in which the government exercises rigid control over the social, economic, and political life, especially by means of a secret police force.

A few weeks ago, a Mississippi teenager was in a courtroom to hear the verdict in a rape case -- hers. Four years ago, when she was eleven, she told her mother that her father had been "sexually fondling" (molesting) her for as far back as she could remember. She also accused him of raping her on one occasion, six months previous to the conversation. Her mother took her to the doctor and to the police. Her father, Marshall Clark, was indicted for sexual abuse, but fled the country and was just recently returned to Mississippi to stand trial. Judge Jerry Terry refused to admit the medical record of the girl's physical injuries (her vagina was torn to her rectum) to the jury because of the time lapse between the attack and the examination. He agreed with her father that there was no way of knowing who the eleven-year-old might have been fooling around with. He declared the psychologist's report irrelevant.

Judge Terry implied that the girl's mother, Lydia Rayner, had staged the whole thing. Look at the kind of woman the mother is! Ms Rayner admits she and her physician husband sheltered Karen Newsom's children while their mother was in jail for contempt of a court order giving the children to their father, who she believed was sexually abusive. She sheltered Dorrie Singley too, the woman who died in hiding while keeping her child from the father she believed to be a child rapist. Ms Rayner was active in MARC (Mothers Against Raping Children) and was suspected of being part of the mothers' underground railroad, under investigation by the FBI for possible conspiracy-kidnapping of other children whose mothers are accusing "innocent" fathers of incest.

Marshall Clark, on the other hand, is an upstanding citizen, a hard worker, a deacon in the

Assembly of God church, whose members attended the trial daily and swore he is "not that kind of man." The only *real* evidence against this man was the word of his daughter. Who can believe the child of such a mother?

When Marshall Clark heard the jury pronounce him "not guilty", he turned around, slowly and deliberately, and smiled at his daughter. She seemed to fly over the benches that separated them, screaming, "You raped me! You raped me." She cried and screamed and pummelled him with her fists. She was forcibly removed from the courtroom and jailed five days for contempt. Her father left the courtroom a free man.

Some might say it is true that anyone could have raped that child during the six months it took her to get up the courage to tell her mother. Some might say that justice would not have been served if the judge had allowed the jury to see the medical records. They might have proved she had been raped, but not by whom. As for the psychologist's report, it would prove even less. There was only the word of a child, and we all know children lie. Ex-wives lie too, are vindictive and hate it when their children's fathers exercise their visitation rights, or so we're told. And, even if a miscarriage of justice did happen in this case, it wasn't intentional, had nothing to do with the nature of the case. It was simply the result of our judicial system's commitment to the principles of "innocent until proven guilty," and guilt "beyond a shadow of a doubt."

The problem with the above reasons, rationalizations, suppositions and scapegoating is their repetition in courts throughout the U.S. In case after case, judges do not believe children when they accuse their fathers of molestation and rape. They usually rule the child is "too young to be reliable," the child gives "confused" testimony or she/he has been "influenced" to give biased testimony. This is what happened in *all* of the recent cases I know of: the Rayner girl; Chrissy Foxworth; Katie and Adam Newsom; Hilary Morgan; Nicole LaLonde; Jesse Murabito's two pre-schoolers; Bethany and Anthony Marks; Lori Brothers; Sherry Neustein. Yet study after study demonstrates that children *do not lie* about sexual abuse. When children report sexual abuse, they tell the truth 98% of the time. In the other 2% of the cases, the children had been abused previously. In addition, recent studies show that relatives commit more sexual child abuse than strangers. According to the Massachusetts Department of Social Services, fathers are the most frequent perpetrators (27.5 percent, strangers (16.8), mother's boyfriend (11.6), stepfathers (11.4), male caretakers (10.1), uncles (9.9), brothers (6.1) and mothers (4.3). Still, judges continue to believe fathers' denials without question.

What this means in real life is that various U.S. judges gave Adam and Katie Newsom to the father of whom Katie said, "Daddy put his pee-pee in my mouth;" gave Chrissy and Nicole and Lauren and all the hundreds of other children whose names and stories we don't know into the hands of the men they say abuse them. It means that all these children are separated from their mothers. Some live full time with the father; some live with him part-time. Others have extended, unsupervised visitation. Some are living in foster homes and the "lucky" ones are underground with mother, family or strangers.

Because judges don't believe children, Elizabeth Morgan was in jail for two years for refusing to give her daughter to the father she believes to be a rapist; Karen Newsom was in for forty-three days; Valerie Marcus was in jail in Oregon; Jesse Murabito was in solitary confinement for seven days; eight months pregnant Lucille Marks was in five days; Virginia LaLonde for nine months; Jean Brothers in almost a year.

Because judges don't believe children, countless mothers have fled with their children and, with help from an "underground railroad" and/or a few trusted family members and friends, attempt to raise their children in a safe home.

Judges don't believe mothers or grandmothers either. Sherri Neustein's grandmother saw her father playing "horsey ride" with the little girl. Becky Marks showed her grandmother how her father put toys into her vagina. All these mothers were told about the abuse of their children, or witnessed it. They acted to protect their children and have been jailed, lost custody and died for their actions, punished by the courts, accused of lying, vindictiveness, child abuse. The stereotype of the bitter, vindictive ex-wife and her mother persecuting the long-suffering husband is alive and well and living in America's courtrooms.

Judges seem unimpressed by medical evidence. Judge Dale, of the Foxworth and Newsom cases, dismissed such evidence as "expressions of suspicion not supported by any factual basis." Yet there is some physical evidence in most cases; torn vaginas, swollen rectums and clitorises, venereal disease. The children describe specific sexual acts forced upon them. If judges are convinced the accused fathers are innocent, why don't they direct the district attorney's office and the police to investigate these crimes? If the fathers didn't rape the children, who did?

The fathers don't ask that question either. They do nothing to find the man who abused their daughters and sons or taught them the words they used to accuse.

Obviously, alleged sexual abuse of one's own children is not treated as a crime in our courtrooms. It is treated as a "custody issue." If Marshall Clark was accused of tearing the vagina of the 11 year old girl next door, would he have been treated so well?

I don't think all judges and other justice officials are child abusers, but I'm sure some are. The latest data I've seen indicate 27 percent of American women and 16 percent of men have been victims of child sexual abuse. Some of their abusers are bound to be judges and their colleagues. I'm sure that some judges use child pornography. I'm sure some judges don't know or believe the statistics about the prevalence of incest. All of this prejudices judges in favor of child sexual abusers.

I think that, given the choice of believing a woman or a child, or believing a man, especially a "respectable" man, judges will usually believe a man.

I believe judges are influenced by our cultural myths about females, sex and incest: that mothers "cause" incest (by coldness, ridicule, indifference, absence), encourage daughters covertly, know and say nothing for economic reasons; that little girls are provocative, seduce their fathers; that incest is harmless and/or enjoyable, and/or good for the girl; that we, females, are responsible for men's sexual response. In other words, they hold preju-dicial beliefs.

It is no accident that mothers are being pun-ished for trying to protect their children. I think this violent response to accusation of child sexual abuse from the justice system is the "official" re-sponse from a nation of men whose women are telling their "dirtiest" secrets. More than twenty-seven percent of America's assaulted daughters are the victims of father rape. Who knew this, before the Women's Liberation Movement got us talking? Not their victims! We were keeping men's secrets for them. "Tell anyone, and some-thing terrible will happen to you," they say. And something terrible *is* happening, and it's happen-ing with the help of the courts!

Incest and other forms of child sexual abuse are the earliest, and the most effective terrorist ac-tions performed by men which ensure women's subjugation. Just think of it, one-fourth of us learned silence and self hatred, and shame and terror at the hands of men who said they loved us, not as adult rape victims, not as battered wives, but as infants in a cradle, as toddlers in the bathtub, as girls on our knees at the side of our beds. No wonder so many of us can't seem to fight for our rights, but seem to accept our place, our role, our subjugation. No wonder we are paralyzed into inaction, so easily discouraged, so ready to attack each other rather than men. Other acts of terrorism are insignificant compared to this, this injury, theft or outright murder of women's spirit. What is an Iranian pipe bomb compared to this terrorism!

Garnett Harrison is the first lawyer in the U. S. to be ordered to jail in child "custody"/child sexual abuse cases. She was under sentence of 30 days in jail and $10,000 fine for organizing an advocacy to free children from their abusers when the legal system failed to protect them. She was the attorney for Lydia Rayner, Dorrie Singley, and Karen Newsom. She is well known throughout Mississippi for her advocacy and action to attain civil rights for *all* citizens. Hollis Watkins, former SNCC field secretary and a leader of Mississippi Rainbow Coalition says, "The struggle we had in the sixties is the same struggle we are fighting here today for Chrissy and Garnett." Exiled from Mississippi, her home and her law practice gone, bankrupt, Garnett founded the CHILDREN'S FREEDOM PROJECT. The project focuses attention on the struggle of women and their children for the right to a safe and secure home. She is available as a lecturer, workshop provider and consultant in child advocacy and as an organizer mobilizing advocates to educate the public that child sexual abuse is a civil rights issue for women and children. You can write for information and to give support and money, to arrange speaking and organizing dates, or to work with her.   Garnett Harrison CHILDREN'S FREEDOM PROJECT, PO Box 1540, Montpelier, VT 05601. January, 1991.

GIRLS AT THE ALTAR *November, 1986*

Sister Rose Edmond, of the Sisters of St. Joseph, was one of my favorite teachers. She taught seventh grade at St. Patrick's grammar school in Astoria, New York City. I loved her. All of her pupils loved her. She responded to our obvious adoration with blushes and smiles and a slight ducking motion of her head which caused her sheer black veil to flutter slightly. I used to touch her veil secretly whenever she walked past my desk. I thought she was beautiful and the most wonderful person I had ever known.

It was during my months with Sister Rose Edmond that I decided to become a nun when I grew up. I too would wear a beautiful habit and live in a house full of women. I would be the teacher of adoring children and, like Sister Rose Edmond, I would let my pupils distract me into

162

telling stories instead of finishing math lessons, or collecting homework, or giving a scheduled test. I would give all the good jobs -- washing the blackboard, cleaning the erasers, decorating the room for holidays, running errands to other rooms or to the convent -- only to the girls, just like she did.

One day a note was sent to our classroom, requesting the immediate attendance of all the boys at a special altar boy meeting in the church. The girls were at least as pleased by this break in routine as the boys. We loved our class time without the boys because Sister would stop whatever we were doing and regale us with stories of her childhood or her experiences in the various convents she had lived in. This time, however, she was just getting started when the boys returned. They didn't burst in and scramble noisily to their seats as they usually did. Instead they marched in proudly and quietly. They were accompanied by Father Vallaci who lined them up along the walls of the room. Father announced, unnecessarily, that the boys had come to show us their new altar boy outfits. We girls filled the room with gasps of pleasure at the sight of such magnificence. The boys had been transformed from those dirty beasts who persecuted us daily into visions of angelic beauty. They were dressed in floor-length, bright red cassocks with mandarin collars and self-covered buttons from collar to hem. Over the cassocks were snowy-white, knee-length surplices, abundantly trimmed in lace at cuff and hem. To complete the costume, large, satin bows, bright red and gorgeous, bloomed at their throats. They were something to see!

When Father was sufficiently satisfied with our admiring responses, he escorted the boys out of the classroom. Sister began telling us about the sacrifices our poor parish had endured in order to raise the money for new vestments for our priests and altar boys, worthy of use on the altar. I hardly heard a word. I was grappling with a new idea, one that was exciting and disturbing. I interrupted her flow of talk with a question.

"Sister, why aren't girls altar boys?"

The look on Sister's face reminded me of the times I asked my Mother questions about something I did not realize was a taboo subject. I could tell that bad news was on its way. She said, "Girls are not altar boys, Marilyn, because only men and boys can serve on the altar." She gave me a sweet look, one intended to get me on her side, to let her answer suffice. I ignored it.

"Sister, why can only men and boys serve on the altar?"

"Because that is the way god wants it," was her weak reply.

"I don't understand," I persisted, noting that the other girls were paying close attention to the exchange. "It doesn't make sense to me." Sister noticed the quiet intensity of the other girls too, so she went on a while about how god called men to the priesthood and wanted women to be sisters, and the different responsibilities they had. I was unimpressed. I thought priests had boring jobs and had no desire to be one. I already knew what sisters did and was going to be one when I grew up. However, I had just developed a burning desire to be an altar boy in the meantime. I wanted to wear those beautiful clothes, to stand before the entire congregation and carry the mass book from one side of the altar to the other. I wanted to walk beside the priest at communion time and hold the gold plate under communicants' chins. I wanted to ring the mass bells! Already I could see myself, kneeling, bent over and praying "MEA CULPA! MEA CULPA!" with the priest, WEARING THOSE SPECTACULAR RED AND WHITE CLOTHES.

Sister realized she had lost me and wasn't doing too well with the other girls either, so she took another tack. She began to speak about the way god had intended things to be, about the god-ordained roles for women and men in the religious life and in the world. She told us that church law forbade women to be in the area of the church around the altar except to clean it or change the altar linens or arrange the altar flowers. Only twice in our lives were we privileged to be invited into the altar space, once when receiving the sacrament of confirmation, and again when we were married at a nuptial mass or took our vows as nuns.

Most of us sat in stunned silence as the import of what Sister was saying sank in. She did not say that girls and women were unclean, that we could contaminate the sacred places, but the message that we were considered unworthy was shockingly clear. My mind began racing. Vinnie

O'Rourke, who played with his little thing in class, was good enough to be an altar boy and stand at the altar, but none of us girls were good enough and NEVER, NEVER, NEVER would be! I was horrified.

"I don't believe it," I stated flatly. "I don't believe it. I don't believe god meant things to be the way you say they are." Sister's voice took on a compassionate tone as she tried to convince and console me. "It is true," she said, "and you will understand and agree with this when you get older."

I was angry and adamant as well as heartsick at Sister's betrayal of us. "I will never agree because you are wrong," I insisted. "If god made us both, than he made girls at least as worthy and important as boys."

"But the church teaches . . . " she began.

"Then the church is wrong," was my reply.

Now Sister was truly upset. She tried to explain why it was impossible for the infallible church to be wrong. But I remained unconvinced. We had reached an impasse. I told her I would think it over, that I knew something was wrong and sooner or later I would figure it out.

Several times after that day, Sister Rose Edmond tried to talk about the subject with me privately. I refused to discuss it. To me, she was no better than my ex-best girlfriend, Mary Lafferty, who told Harry La Mott that I liked him, even though she swore she wouldn't. Like Mary, Sister had sided with the boys. I felt betrayed. How could I trust her after that? I assuaged my broken heart by transferring my affection to Sister William Agnes, but nothing healed the pain I felt everytime I saw the boys at the altar in their red cassocks.

THE POWER OF NAMING *February 1991*

When I see a photograph of a naked woman tied up so that movement would cause strangling, her eyes covered by a rag, her face expressionless, as if she is unconscious or drugged, the suggestion of a rumpled sheet in the background, I think she was photographed just as her assailant was about to pick her up and toss her into the trunk of his car. However, the context of this photograph, as illustration for an article in the Los Angeles **Lesbian News** about a Lesbian sex photographic exhibit, is supposed to correct my false impression. According to the photographer, *this* photograph of a naked woman, hog-tied and seemingly drugged, is a photograph of a woman, a Lesbian, in a "sexual situation."

What am I supposed to do with this contradiction? I feel emotionally manipulated. This is not a kids' puzzle, a "What is wrong with this picture?" photo. What does the photographer want from me? Does she want me to respond as a Lesbian who is sexual, to pay attention to my sexual response to this photo of a bound woman engaged in a "sexual situation?" I can't do it. My original response remains. I put the paper away

167

for a while, then return to it. My feelings don't change. I feel manipulated, tricked, annoyed. The woman remains the image of an unconscious victim of male violence. I don't see her as engaged in Lesbian sexual activity, am not able to draw the line, to say this is a Lesbian sexual situation I don't want to add to my sexual repertoire.

Finally, it occurs to me that my confusion is caused by *my* unquestioned agreement with the photographer that the "situation" of a trussed, naked woman is "sexual." Why must I accept the description of the photograph as one of "Lesbian sex." If she included a photo of a smiling, naked woman tied to a tree and bleeding from razor cuts over her body, would I be obliged to agree to a Lesbian sexual interpretation of the situation? Asking these questions sparked a question I haven't thought to ask during more than ten years of discourse about Lesbian sadomaschism. If Lesbians in the photographs describe their "situations" as "sexual," do I have an obligation to expand my definitions and interpretations of Lesbian sexual activity to include theirs?

Acting out scenes of dominance/submission, which can include bondage and "discipline," dressing up in leather, in uniforms or in costumes are some of the activities which are named *sadomasochism* by women and men who say they willingly participate in such activities. Sadomasochistic vocabulary, costumes, scripts and behaviors are much the same, at least in the U.S., no matter what the sex or the sexual preference of the participants. However, the central fact of sadomasochism is that, no matter what their sex or sexual preference, sadists say they experience pleasure from the infliction of abuse and pain, while masochists say they experience pleasure from receiving abuse and pain. I have no problem accepting the term *sadomasochism* for these activities and feeling states. My hesitation comes from my inability to conceive of sadomasochistic practices as sexual activity, an inability which is intensified when they are described as expressions of Lesbian sexuality.

For years, I have listened to Lesbians say that criticism of their sadomasochistic practices and displays are no different from criticism of Lesbian sexuality by the non-Lesbian majority. Concerns about perceived violence in sadomasochism are buried under the concepts of mutual consent and trust, or shamed away by charges of prudishness and a lack of sexual imagination. These responses from sadomasochists have led to an uneasy acceptance of sadomasochism by Lesbians who don't really approve of sadomasochism, but who don't want to behave like our oppressors do. They have also led to a silencing of Lesbians' critical thinking on the subject. About the only way criticism of sadomasochism can be voiced is to say that the sight and sounds of consensual bondage and discipline, the blood and bruises, the chains, dog collars and swastikas are upsetting to Lesbians who have suffered non-consensual bondage, discipline and the rest. Lesbian sadomasochists can then be asked to "be discreet," to be sensitive to their sisters' protection needs, or, can be told not to display sadomasochistic paraphernalia in particular Lesbian "public" space.

Meditating on the photograph of a hog-tied woman has freed me from those constraints. I no longer have to betray all I know from my experiences of bodily pain, of emotional abuse, of humiliation, of dominance and submission, as well as all I know from my experiences of sexual arousal, play, ecstasy, by accepting the definition of sadomasochist behaviors as sexual. I remember when rape was "sex," was "love," was "wanted," was "women's fault," was "playing around." I rejected these definitions and interpretations because they did not describe my rape experiences or those of other raped women and children. This process of feminist re-naming and re-interpreting our experiences to correct the lies and distortions of patriarchy has been going on for years, is far from over. I want to continue the process by refusing to accept, as descriptions of reality, the current words, interpretations and definitions of sadomasochism. These were originally developed by rich, white men to erase, distort and camouflage their ritualized torture of women, and legitimized by Freud's pronouncement that women are masochistic by nature. The fact that some Lesbians have adopted similar behaviors and language is beside the point. I can and do reject their description of sadomasochistic activities as Lesbian sex, as Lesbian sexual situations.

Some people are sexually aroused by applause for their acting or their touchdowns. Some people are aroused by the sight of something beautiful, some by music, some by food. Some people are turned on by the non-consensual use of whips and chains, some by skinning cats or setting fires, some by the sight of naked children. Ordinarily, these are not considered sexual activities, sexual situations. Photographs of Lesbians in these situations would not be included in a Lesbian sex exhibit. Can't I argue logical consistency for refusing to name the acts of tying a woman to a tree and then cutting her with a razor, sexual acts -- even though some women and men are sexually aroused by the activities? I believe I can.

Now I can say that some Lesbians can only participate in sexual activity, or simply enjoy sexual activity more, when such activity is accompanied by some form of sadomasochistic behaviors, just as I can say that some Lesbians can only participate in sexual activity, or simply enjoy sex more, when they are drinking or stoned. Just as we exclude drinking alcohol, smoking marijuana or taking drugs from our definitions of Lesbian sex, even when they are accompanied by sexual activity, so we can exclude sadomasochism from definitions of Lesbian sex.

Once we separate sadomasochism from Lesbian sexual behavior, we can talk about Lesbian sadomasochism in the same tone, and with the same concern for the wellbeing of our sisters, as we show for our sisters for whom drugs and alcohol are necessities. We have learned to tell other Lesbians that we do not approve of, or that we are concerned about, or that we are offended by or that we will not allow in our homes, establishments, Lesbian public spaces, their use of cigarettes, marijuana, meat, drugs, alcohol, violence. We can learn to speak our real feelings about sadomasochism, too. We can ask ourselves if we are *enablers*, when we remain silent in the presence of Lesbians on leashes, of Lesbians with clothespins clipped to their nipples, of Lesbians wearing handcuffs and carrying whips. When Lesbians extol the highs of sadomasochism, we can listen with the understanding learned from sisters extolling the joys of "partying," who also named us prudes and faint-hearted for eschewing alcohol, drugs, and other mind-altering substances and behaviors. We may even be able to ask how "consensual" is the consent of a Lesbian whose life has taught her to thank the person who ties and beats and cuts and pees on her body! Separating sadomasochism from Lesbian sexuality allows us to understand sadomasochism and to name it as one of the more obvious self-hating, body-hating methods women use to act out the pain we all suffered growing up female -- and as we know, there's nothing "sexy" about that pain!

V. The Personal Is Political

MOTHER OF THE GROOM *January, 1985*

I did not go to my son's wedding. The decision shattered the trust that had been building between us, and between me and the woman with whom he was sharing his life. Before they married, they treated me and my companion lover with affection and respect. We could talk with humor and without inhibitions on a wide range of subjects, agreeing and disagreeing without rancor. Work, distance and finances kept us from seeing each other often; but we kept in touch by letter and phone. While not idyllic, our relationship was a good one, and I was pleased and relieved that his attitude toward my Lesbian life was a positive one.

I did not want to stay away from the ceremony. I did not want to miss an important event in the life of my child. I did not want him to suffer shame or embarrassment on my account, having to explain his mother's absence from his wedding. Even more heartfelt was my desire to avoid another emotional debacle with one of my offspring. Over the years, I had achieved a more or less easy peace with all four of my adult children; and I dreaded any resumption of trouble with my thirty-year-old eldest child and only son. Yet once again, I was in a no-win "mother dilemma," a not uncommon place for mothers of adult children, especially Lesbian mothers. If I went to the wedding, I would not be at peace with myself. If I did not go to the wedding, I would not be at peace with him. And no matter what the decision, I would feel guilty about it. After all, what kind of a mother has to stop and think about whether or not to attend her child's wedding? A Lesbian mother does!

My son and his companion lover are conscious persons. For three years before the wedding they lived together as a non-conforming heterosexual couple in a committed, monogamous relationship. During those years they paid the price for living an affectional-sexual relationship outside the socially sanctioned, state *licensed* and state supported affectional-sexual relationship: the institution of marriage. Their life, health, auto insurance, their credit records, tax returns, airline tickets were those of two single persons, not those of a couple. They could not automatically inherit from each other, or speak for each other in case of a medical emergency. When visiting family, they had the problem of sleeping arrangements. They lived with the social awkwardness that comes from existing outside the language and therefore having no word, no term which correctly described each other or their relationship to each other or to outsiders. Many of these problems are the problems experienced by Lesbian and Gaymen couples, problems my companion lover and I shared with them.

Certainly they had their heterosexual privilege. They could be affectionate in public. They could talk about their lives together, even to people who would think they were "living in sin." They never feared losing their jobs or being publicly humiliated should their relationship "be discovered." They were accepted in most places and by most people as a couple, one who would eventually "do the right thing," and marry.

They vigorously resisted the pressure to marry. She was afraid she'd turn into a wife, and so was he. He was afraid he'd turn into a husband, and so was she. They disapproved of marriage, said it institutionalized the inequality of women. They said the state exceeded its power over the lives of citizens by licensing marriage, by which it was "legalizing" the sexual and reproductive activity of certain LICENSED women and men couples only, and "legitimating" the children resulting from that licensed sexual coupling. They deplored what they saw as the collusion of the state with religion by its licensing of cohabitation/sexual activity between women and men couples only, thus giving all same-sex couples' cohabitation/sexual activity the status of illegal, illicit, SIN, in spite of any consenting adults statutes the state might have passed. They stood with Lesbians and Gaymen in their opposition to institutionalized heterosexuality.

Need I say that I was proud of the male child I had raised, that I approved of his choice of companion lover, that I supported them in their efforts to live their beliefs? I was shocked when they told me they had decided to get married. They said they were not giving in to pressure. They said they no longer feared becoming a wife or a husband. They were confident the marriage ceremony would not disrupt the habits of equality their lives together had developed. They were tired of the aggravation and the hassle, personal and financial, they suffered because they were an unmarried couple. They said they were sorry for all the distress they were causing other family members by their refusal to marry. What's the harm, really, in saying a few words in public, words they had said to each other privately many times. And yes, since they were going to do it, they might as well get a license. And yes, the ceremony would be performed by a person with a license to perform legal marriages; and yes, there would be engraved wedding invitations, wedding showers, wedding gifts, and wedding guests. But the bride would not vow obedience, nor would she wear white!

How could the mother of the groom attend such a ceremony, a ceremony which celebrates the institution which is the cornerstone of her past oppression as a married woman, and her present oppression as a Lesbian? How could I participate in a ceremony by which the child of my body acted out his informed consent to the right of the state to declare his relationship with his companion lover lawful, legal, and by default, to declare my relationship with my companion lover out-of-the-law, illegal? I could not.

So here we are four years later. I feel rejected by my first born; and he feels rejected by his mother. I also feel jealousy, guilt, resentment, and a host of other not-so-nice feelings about our present relationship. It does not help to know that I "did the right thing." The "personal" may be "political," but when we act politically instead of personally with our children, they usually punish us for it. Mothers are not supposed to have principles that conflict with our mandate to love our children unconditionally.

Yet men who abhor sexism do not join organizations which deny membership to women. White people who abhor racism do not join organizations which deny membership to people of color. Christians, believers and non-believers, who abhor anti-Semitism do not join organizations which deny membership to Jews. The refusal to join organizations which deny membership, and the benefits accruing to members, to others because of sex, race, religion, and so on, is the very least that can be expected of those who profess belief in equality and civil rights for all.

What would we think of a man who called himself a feminist, said he supported the equal rights amendment and the concept of comparable worth, and then asked his women friends to attend the ceremony initiating him into a prestigious men-only club? I'm sure we would not only seriously doubt his commitment to women's equality, but would also consider his invitation an insult. And yet the families and friends of Lesbians and Gaymen continue to join the largest social organization in the world, the most prestigious one, the one every one is expected to join, the one with the greatest amount of government subsidies and supports, the voluntary association which prohibits membership to Lesbians and Gaymen: the institution of marriage. Their disregard of our feelings, as well as our rights, is so profound that they add insult to injury by inviting us to attend those rites which are denied us. They expect us to congratulate them, to throw a party on their behalf, to act as their maid of honor/bridesmaid or best man/usher -- and in some cases, want us to leave our companion lovers at home while we do.

The families and friends of Lesbians and Gaymen are asking us to collude in our oppression when they ask, insist, that we participate in their marriage rites. It is in their best interests, and in the best interests of patriarchy, when we do what they wish. Our part in their marriage rites allows them to deny us our rites/rights with an easy conscience. It allows them to continue to believe that we believe they deserve the pomp and the ceremony and the privileges that go with them, that we, the "deviant," are satisfied with the crumbs from their tables, with our broomstick weddings.[7] It is way past the time for Lesbians and Gaymen to begin disturbing the consciences of our families and friends, especially those of our children. As long as we are denied participation in what is called the "honorable state of matrimony," it is no honor to be called Mother of the Groom.

PRETTY IN PINK *July, 1986*

At a recent Lesbian event, I saw two women wearing T-shirts that disturbed me. One proclaimed, LESBIANS FOR LIPSTICK, and the other announced, DYKES FOR SPIKES. Now why would Lesbians display such slogans at a Lesbian event? Their shirts didn't have brand names on them, Revlon or Kinney's for example, so they weren't advertising lipstick or high heeled shoes for a manufacturer or a retailer. If I had seen the women wearing the T-shirts at work or at the market, I might have assumed that they were telling people that Lesbians do/can/should-have-the- right-to wear lipstick and high heels, but since only Lesbians were present, that assumption made no sense. I didn't know there was any move afoot to deny anyone access to these items.

Societies, generally, have customs and laws that more or less rigidly define which clothing and other body adornments are appropriate for women and for men. Societies, generally, punish members of either sex who adopt all or some of the clothing and adornments of the other, or who do not wear the clothing and adornments considered proper for their sex. This punishment can be institutionalized and as severe as death, torture, branding, shock treatment, or it can be informal and result only in being ridiculed and shunned as unmarriageable, unattractive or queer. As with

179

most customs and laws, those regarding the proper body adornment for women and men are unevenly applied. For example, in the forties and fifties when women (meaning Lesbians) were required to wear at least three items of female attire or risk arrest, I was going to the grocery store in a man's shirt and jeans, wearing unisex-looking loafers and no bra or cosmetics, unknowingly protected by heterosexual privilege. Of course when I got "dressed up," my body was appropriately covered by a dress, lipstick and high heeled shoes.

In the USA, the use of lipstick by women has been more or less mandatory only since the forties. I remember how embarrassed I felt then, going lipstick-less to St. Agnes High School in the morning, and how skilled I became, after school, at applying lipstick while standing in a moving bus with twenty pounds of textbooks in my arms. I felt "undressed" without lipstick for years after. The phrase women frequently use for applying make-up, "putting on my face," indicates how much a part of our bodies cosmetics have become.

When the second wave of the Women's Liberation Movement hit, women, many of them Lesbians, began to critique our use of make-up. Why do women wear make-up? Why do we pay so much attention to our faces, cover our facial skin, our lips, our eye lids, brows, lashes with artificial color, carry mirrors and cosmetics wherever we go, frequently "repair the damage" caused by eating and drinking, by kissing, by time? Is being a woman not so much a biological reality as a role or an act for which make-up (make-believe?) is required?

In the USA at present, women are expected to wear face make-up. As women we are supposed to wear more or less make-up depending upon the time, place and occasion for our display, and, for non-Lesbian women, depending upon the preference of the individual man the woman hopes to please.

Men like women to wear make-up because they feel flattered knowing that all the women they see wearing make-up, wear it to please men. Men like us to wear make-up because it helps to hide our common humanity, makes us look like "not-men." Make-up sets women apart from men. It reminds men that we are not to be taken seriously, that the real purpose for our existence is sex, reproduction and service.

Without lipstick the size and shape and texture of women's lips are not different from those of men. With lipstick, our lips become women's lips, sexy lips, what cosmetic companies' ads promise they will be: wet, glossy, luscious; wet, smooth, moist; wet, hot, inviting. The words and the pictures that accompany cosmetic ads are intended to reinforce the idea of women's lips as sex organs, rather than organs of speech, reminding men of those other lips of ours, those hidden lips. . . and fellatio.

Historically, high-heeled shoes have been worn by women and men, usually to flaunt the indolence that wealth provides. At present, some men wear higher heels on their footwear in order to appear taller or because of their work, riding and roping horses, for example.

Women in the USA have been expected to wear high-heeled shoes when we dress for certain occupations. One reason for this practice is that the legs of women and men are not very different in appearance in their natural state. High-heels change the shape of the calf muscles and thus of the legs. When sheer stockings were invented, the hair on women's legs had to go, too. Voila! Women's legs were now things to be whistled at and photographed and immortalized in concrete. Women in "sensible" shoes were ridiculed, old maids or worse. Nowadays, women can wear sensible shoes for exercise and walking, and are "suspect" only when we wear them when we are supposed to be "on display."

High-heels on shoes cause women to walk with a certain tentativeness, a cautiousness that is lacking when each foot can be put solidly on the ground. We give the appearance of fragility, vulnerability in high heels, evoking in men a desire to protect us, to offer their arm -- or to take advantage of our diminished mobility.

Wearing high-heeled shoes forces our feet into an unnatural position for walking and causes pain and injury to various body parts. Wearing high-heeled shoes causes callouses on the balls of the feet, corns, bunions, ingrown toenails, shortened tendons, weakened ankles, and back and spine ailments. Their wear causes turned ankles, falls and other accidents to the wearer. I suggest we look at the bare feet of old women at the beach to see the damage their shoes have done, if our own feet do not yet show the scars.

This emphasis on our appearance, not just make-up and shoes, but our hair and clothing, our posture, gestures, walk, facial expressions, the size and shape of our body, our breasts, causes all of us to be conscious of our appearance most of the time.

Because as women we are sex objects to men, no matter whatever else we are to them, we have the tricky job of trying to appear as if we are *not* sex objects in inappropriate situations. Women usually do not want to be perceived primarily as sex objects when they go to work, for example, or if they must rush to the hospital emergency room, or report a rape, or purchase an automobile, or apply for a teaching assistantship.

The task of wearing "man-pleasing" clothing, make-up, jewelry, of looking like a woman trying to please men, while not encouraging the un-wanted sexual attention of men, is particularly tricky for Lesbians who "pass" as heterosexual.

Women's felt "need" for products which create the illusion that they look very different from men, products that allow women to paint, pluck, cream, moisten, brush, cut, file, remove, alter their body parts result in a cosmetic industry with profits in the billions of dollars. I don't know how much more of our money we give to men's med-ical industry by attempts to alter our bodies surgi-cally, or by the illnesses and accidents and allergies we incur from all of the above.

I know how hard it is to change our attitudes about how we look. It's been easier for women to change how we think and feel about women's intelligence, physical strength, leadership ability, courage, power, talent, integrity, nature, instincts, than it has been to change how we think and feel about our physical appearance. No woman is ever satisfied with how she looks. In the USA a woman IS her looks. All else is secondary. It was easy enough for me to quit wearing high-heels. I ruined my feet trying to wear them when I was an adolescent and for years I looked in vain for "dressy" shoes with low heels. Make-up was not so easy to do without. I loved the way I looked in make-up. I was vain about my eyes in particular, and only was reconciled to my own bare face when I paid attention to the different ways men treated me when I wore make-up, and when I did not. And I must confess that I have never learned to love the hair on my legs.

Of course, men and most women do not believe that women who wear lipstick and high-heels are Lesbians anyway. So wearing lipstick and high-heels insures that others will think we are heterosexual, in addition to the other results of their wear noted above. Could those T-shirted Lesbians be suggesting that the rest of us go out of our way to pass as heterosexual by wearing heels and lipstick?

Some Lesbians say they have transcended the sexism in the USA, at least in their personal choices, and feel "free" to choose to behave in ways that are still coercive and mandatory in the lives of other, less enlightened, less conscious, man-pleasing women. They tell me that they can wear the make-up and high-heeled shoes and pretty dresses. Their spirits are free. They tell me that the Women's Liberation Movement was about women having choices. "Personal freedom" is a particularly American myth, one that has co-opted and diluted every movement for social change in this country including ours. When Lesbians look like, walk like, dress like the property of men, in a society where all women are assumed to be the property of men, how will we and our sisters know what a free woman looks like?

FEMALE FURY:
we have our reasons *October, 1989*

Yearly, as the weather gets hot and then hotter, as the perspiration forms under my breasts, as I witness human males of every age strolling by dressed only in their shoes and short-shorts, a T-shirt hanging from a pocket ready for use should the weather change or the stroller feel the urge to pop in somewhere for a bite to eat, I suffer attacks of fevered female fury. I HATE it that men can walk the streets so skimpily dressed, getting optimum benefit from the cooling breeze, while women must cover our breasts or risk arrest, ridicule and a number of other unpleasantries. I am too hot to stroll. I walk while trying to coax some breeze through the armholes of my tank top by holding my arms out from my sides and raising them above my head now and then. I walk scowling. I want to stand on street corners and harangue. I want to shout at men! "Put your shirt on or else I'll. . . ." I'll what? I'll be carried off by police, one more deranged woman walking the streets and muttering threats, that's what!

One would think, considering all I know of women's oppression, that I could get through the summer without letting this minor form of it get under my sweaty skin. Women say, "Even if it was legal, I wouldn't go bare-breasted. They would still snicker and make remarks." I say, "That is *not* the point. Male power is the point! Patriarchy is the point!" It seems illogical for a society to allow men to go naked from the waist up in public, while forbidding that degree of nudity to women (except in licensed establishments where clothed men go to see breasts for entertainment). In many places, women may not bare a breast to feed their nursing young! Men, for no reason but their comfort, and because they have the institutionalized power to do so, give only to themselves the right to display their naked breasts. Why not us?

Well, as we all know, in our country men are sexually sensitive to the sight of female breasts, even when the breasts are covered. When the breasts are naked, the sight is supposed to drive men into a sexual frenzy. We also know that their arousal must be satisfied or something terrible happens to their private parts. Because the female who "causes" sexual arousal in a male is the one who is supposed to take care of it for him (hence the "she made me do it," defense in the Garden of Eden and in rape, molestation, harassment outrages), the public nature of the arousal becomes a problem for men. They solve it by making us cover up in public, with no thought to our comfort.

I suppose they don't want other men to see the naked breasts of "their" women (because of the reason above). Also, seeing naked breasts all the time might spoil the titillation they get in sneaking a peek down the front of a blouse, in flipping through the pages of porno magazines, in speculating and fantasizing about the covered breasts of the women around them. Since they are in charge of women's bodies, why not make us dress in ways that please them! This absurd exercise of male privilege occurs unnoticed by most men and by many women and girls. Of course, once it is pointed out to sweaty females, we notice and never forget. That is why I've always been an admirer of Nikki Craft. She is notorious for taking her blouse off in public places and getting arrested and going to jail for that affront to public decency. She always makes a big fuss about this unequal treatment of women and men, gets in the paper and on television. Lots of women have their consciousness raised through her efforts. Nikki Craft is another one of our "wild woman" activists who enriches our struggle to eliminate the power men/patriarchy have over the bodies of women. I always think of her in August and wish her well.

CINDERELLA'S SISTERS   *October, 1984*

At a meeting, a Lesbian I had not seen in a year stood to make an announcement. She resembled the skeletal survivors of Hitler's camps. Her bones showed through her skin everywhere. Her face was almost fleshless; her cheeks were gone; her once sweet smile was a bizarre contortion. She was extolling the good work of "overeaters" anonymous groups for the "control" of body weight and of "eating disorders." Later she told me she "chose" to be "thin," that she liked the feeling of "lightness."

Next day, in one of life's macabre coincidences, I learned that an acquaintance of mine, a woman in her sixties, had recently died of starvation. She had been a dancer, a showgirl in her youth and hated her older, heavier body. She was on a protein drink diet when she died. I do not know if she died thin.

My mother just celebrated her eighty-first birthday. She is an artist and a full-time college student. She starts each day with thirty-five minutes of yoga exercises. She no longer eats breakfast, bread, starchy vegetables, desserts, but she is unable to lose another pound. She admits to feeling deprived, but believes that sooner or later she will "slim" to a size twelve, her still unreachable goal after a lifetime of dieting.

During my high school days, Marion Marquarte ate a three-scoop ice cream cone every day after lunch whether she wanted it or not. She was what we called in those days "painfully thin." She did not gain an ounce. Joan Quinn and I, guiltily eating a single-scooper once a week, envied her malady. Rosie, my coffee-klatch neighbor when I was a housewife, used whipping cream in her coffee and on her cereal. She drank a chocolate milkshake every afternoon, too. She was trying to gain weight because she was too thin. She wore size seven clothes and usually shopped in the girls' department since women's clothes were not made in such small sizes then. I sometimes think of her when shopping. Now "women's" clothes start at size three and end at twelve or fourteen. Anything larger is in fat lady departments and fat lady stores.

I have been dieting or not dieting for as long as I can remember, but my dieting began in earnest when I was eighteen and expecting my first child. It was a well-established pattern of behavior by the time my fourth and last child was born six years later. My doctor said I should not gain weight while pregnant or at any other time. The "small portion of lean meat/fish accompanied by leafy vegetables and fresh fruit" diet regimes were beyond my financial means, so I relied on the least expensive weight loss diet - not eating. My doctor dispensed vitamins to keep me and the fetuses healthy while I starved. He also dispensed a diet drug, Preludin, to keep me from feeling too hungry and to supply the energy I needed for the eighteen-hour a day, seven days a week schedule I worked in those days. Still, I was not thin. "Not fat" was the best I could do.

For years, my diet was the first thing I thought about when I awoke. If I was not dieting, I began the day feeling guilty. If I was dieting, I felt virtuous, but aggrieved. "Why me?" My life was a cycle of losing weight until I could no longer stand the diet pill feeling, then slowly gaining back the weight - plus a little more - when I ate "normally." Then came the disgusted phase, chiding myself for lacking the "willpower" to do without food. A trip to the doctor for a check-up (fortunately I was always in excellent health) and a new prescription and I was dieting again. Each time I needed to diet more stringently to lose weight. "The older you get, the harder it is to lose weight," they say.

Every woman I knew, except Rosie, lived the same diet life as I did. We never stayed the same weight ever. We were in good health, but all of us were "overweight" according to our doctors and the articles we read and the images we saw in magazines, movies, television. It never occurred to us to question the diet cycle. After all, our doctors recommended it. We could not ask questions like: Is dieting harmful to my health? Is "overweight" really a health problem? We had not ever thought to ask about the diet pills! It took the Black Power, Anti-war and Women's Liberation movements to shake our faith in established, hierarchical authority of all kinds, including that of the medical profession.

I went from a believing Catholic housewife and mother, the pillar of my parish, to a radical Lesbian feminist on the cutting edge of the movements for institutional and personal change during those years. I learned to analyze, organize, speak out and write. I was overjoyed to recognize and be freed from beliefs and attitudes and behaviors which oppressed me. I was even willing, albeit not so joyfully, to recognize and begin the process of freeing myself from beliefs, attitudes and behaviors of mine which oppressed others. But, in 1975, when members of Fat Underground wrote and spoke about the ways that they/we/I were duped by doctors and the diet industry, I got mad at the women who brought me the bad news. I hugged my calorie counter to my politically correct chest and stated firmly, "Now you are going too far!"

How's this for resistance! I was ready to believe every medical horror story that came flooding from the mouths of women too long silenced by the belief in "God the Doctor." I knew about unnecessary surgery, involuntary sterilization, abortion butchery, electric shock, "cures" for Lesbianism, doctor-induced tranquilizer addiction. By this time, I even knew about the dangers of diet pills. Yet, knowing all this, I was not willing to know that the doctors and the diet industry were wrong and knew they were wrong about weight loss, about "over-eating" and "overweight" and about "normal" size. I did not want to know that dieting resulted in greater weight gain, that the more I dieted the less likely I was to become and remain thin. I was not willing to be freed from my fantasy that someday, somehow, someway, Marilyn Murphy would be healthily thin, beautifully thin, forever thin and not hungry!

I am not sure that I have completely exorcized my thin Marilyn fantasy. I have allowed myself to see the truth I always "knew" from my life experiences, the truth the doctors, the diet industry and the cult of thin female beauty contradicted by their authority and their greed and their ever-presence in our daily life. This truth is slowly finding its way from fat liberation publications to medical journals to popular magazines. This truth:

1. When I eat "normally," neither gaining nor losing weight, I must eat much less than most "naturally" thin women I know.

2. To lose weight, I must eat much, much less than my thin friends who go on diets to lose the "five pounds I gained on my vacation."

3. To gain weight, all I have to do is eat a regular breakfast regularly.

4. Every time I lose weight by dieting, I regain it, plus a little more, when I begin to eat "normally."

5. Every time I diet I must eat less than before in order to lose; and I must eat less when I eat "normally" to maintain a weight loss.

6. Most of my life, I have been hungry most of the time.

The myth that thin is beautiful, normal and healthy for everyone is just now being challenged. Scientists are now proving that diets do cause people to gain weight, that our dieting bodies react to food loss as if we were starving. This is logical when we realize that nine hundred calories a day is the World Health Council definition of starvation. Bodies don't know we are trying to wear size ten jeans. Deprive the body of food and she begins to use the easily available energy stored in the heart, muscles, brain. After four to six weeks, the body taps its energy reserves in the fat cells. It also slows down our systems to conserve as much of that reserve energy as possible in case this food loss emergency is a long one. When the body again has access to food, it replaces the depleted emergency energy reserves (fat cells), adding some extra in preparation for another "famine." This cycle is repeated with each "famine-diet," and is not good for our health.

Doctors still put women on diets, however. They still surgically remove intestines or half of the stomach from healthy "fat" women. They wire women's jaws shut and sell them liquid protein drinks. They perfected a new technique to melt fat and vacuum it from our bodies. They are not deterred by knowing that our fat produces estrogen when our ovaries shut down, improving the health of menopausal and post-menopausal women.

Aided and abetted by our doctors, American women are encouraged to emulate Cinderella's sisters, mutilating our bodies for beauty's sake.

Given the choice, many, many dieting women would rather be dead than fat -- and so they may be.

For our health's sake, and for our happiness, I urge all women to read and pass on *Shadow on a Tightrope* edited by Schoenfelder and Wieser, Spinsters/Aunt Lute Book Company, PO Box 410687, San Francisco, CA 94141.

LESBIANS WHO GO BACK TO MEN
and other strange occurrences *February, 1983*

Feminists are fond of saying we should trust our feelings; we should "go with" our feelings. I have trouble with these ideas because I've learned that not all of my feelings can be trusted. As a female, the oldest child in a large, poor, Catholic family, I grew up with two overriding feelings: a (overdeveloped) sense of responsibility and (irrational) guilt. I was thirty-five years old before I more or less got some control over guilt. But I still have a lot of trouble with feelings of responsibility. I have yet to go to a meeting of any sort where I don't feel an almost irresistible urge to volunteer for something.

The point of all this is that feelings, like food preferences or standards of beauty and behavior, are culture-based. We are trained to feel the feelings appropriate to our sex, race, religion, class and whatever other category a culture deems important. We are taught the appropriate labels for feelings; and we are taught to repress culturally inappropriate feelings. Further, we are taught that culturally approved feelings are "natural," are "human nature," that all other feelings are perversions of the "natural." This training is an essential part of social cohesiveness, conformity, and control.

Because women are expected to love, honor, and serve men in our private and our public lives, we are trained to feel guilt, shame, and an assortment of other nasty feelings if our feelings cause us to desire to live with and love women instead of men. The power of anti-Lesbian feelings within women who feel drawn to women is proven by the vast majority of Lesbians who have "tried men:" that is, who have dated men, had sex with men, lived with men, married men, before they were able to live Lesbian lives.

In order to live happily as a Lesbian, a woman must do something about the Lesbian-negative feelings she has developed living in this culture. She cannot "trust" those feelings, or "go with" them, not if she hopes to trust and go with her positive feelings of love and sexual desire for women. If she doesn't resolve this conflict of feelings, she will not act on her Lesbian feelings, or she will act on them as a guilt-ridden, ashamed-of-herself Lesbian. Fortunately, most Lesbians resolve this conflict by overcoming their Lesbian-negative feelings. If, once in a while, we experience a momentary recurrence of those negative feelings, we don't burn our "warm, fuzzy, dyke"

T-shirt. We dismiss them and go about our business.

But what about the Lesbian who says she has met a wonderful, "special" man for whom she has strong feelings? She thinks she should go with these feelings. When I express horror at the prospect, she says I am no better than the Jerry Falwells who do not want us to act on our Lesbian feelings. This line of reasoning is the result of faulty logic. Living a Lesbian life is good for women. Lesbians are physically and mentally healthier, are happier, more self-reliant, more independent, enjoy higher self-esteem and a more satisfying sex life than women who relate to men. In addition, relating to men is dangerous. Women who relate to men suffer physical, mental, emotional, and spiritual abuse regularly. Even those "special" men we hear about drain a woman's energy, insult her intelligence and expect her to serve them as their "privileged domestic" (a term I've stolen from Dr. Joyce Brothers who coined it in her 1984 book on men).

I think that a Lesbian who finds herself attracted to men could use the experience to better understand her still-enslaved, non-Lesbian sisters; but it is not in her best interest to go with the feeling. That is worse for her than going back to cigarettes; the odds of harm coming to her body are higher with men!

I apply the same reasoning to feelings of sexual sadism and masochism. Some Lesbians go with those feelings by incorporating humiliation, physical pain, verbal abuse and bondage into their

196

sexual activity. This, too, is harmful to their physical, mental, emotional and spiritual health. Play-acting "scenes" which parody the sadism inflicted upon women, children, people of color, Jews, disabled and poor people, desensitizes the actors to the real humiliation, physical pain, verbal abuse and bondage suffered by all people in the bottom roles of our society. In similar ways, children are desensitized to the horrors of war and other kinds of violence by playing war, cops and robbers, and cowboys and "Indians." Here again, feelings can't be trusted. Like feelings for men, these feelings, if acted upon, can put women in danger.

I believe feelings are not a mandate for action.. (Certainly women would be safer if MEN quit acting on their culturally-rewarded feelings of violence toward women.) None of us act on all our feelings ever. We constantly make judgements about which feelings to go with and which to leave at the feeling stage. How often would we go to work if we only went when we "felt like it?" How often do we remain silent when we want so much to tell off a boss, a traffic cop, a customer? We try not to act on anti-Semitic, racist, ageist feelings. We try to control feelings of jealousy and anger. Our desire to do what we think is right/ethical and our need for safety frequently controls our desires to behave in inappropriate or dangerous ways.

How about making them a mandate for action!

AND BABY MAKES TWO *Sept/Oct., 1986*

For years I've been thinking of writing about motherhood; and now that many Lesbians are seriously considering motherhood as an option for themselves, a thoughtful article on that subject by a Lesbian who has mothered for thirty-five years seems timely. I have four children, three females and one male, aged twenty-nine to thirty-five at this writing. I am also a daughter, the eldest child of a mother whose behavior I have been scrutinizing for fifty-four years. I am a grandmother to five, going-on-six, grandchildren as well.

Motherhood is an experience so mystified by folklore and superstition, by science and religion, by womb-envy and woman-hating, that most women, at least in this culture, become mothers without really knowing what they are getting into. The people who could bring a little light to the subject, mothers ourselves, are silenced or discredited by the very forces which mystified our experience. It is absolutely unacceptable for mothers to question the motherhood imperative or to point out the difficulties inherent in motherhood unless we include the obligatory disclaimer, "Oh, but it was worth it!" To omit the disclaimer is to risk censure as a bad mother, a bitter mother, a cold mother, a mother who does not love her own children. I have never written anything as anxiety producing as this essay because I know what many readers of this piece will think that of me. And what of my children? Will they be angry with me when they read this? Will they think I do not love them? Will they reject me? The first draft of this article had defensive, "I'm really a good mother" phrases scattered throughout it. Only my commitment to write the truth as I have experienced it has kept me writing about motherhood in spite of my sweaty palms.

I ask Lesbians why they are choosing to become mothers. I know why I chose to become a mother. I believed that my "vocation," that is, my calling, my mission from "god," was motherhood, not the convent life which was my original goal. I was only fifteen at the time I came to this realization, so I do not judge myself harshly for not thinking more clearly. But nowadays, women in their thirties, independent women, Lesbian women are choosing to have babies. Why?

It is not surprising, of course, that so many Lesbians are choosing to have babies now that artificial insemination is available to unmarried women. Lesbians are always in the forefront of revolutionary societal changes, and motherhood independent of men is one of those changes. Still, after the revolutionary conception, the result is quite commonplace. It is simply one more woman having a baby, and there has been nothing very revolutionary about that event, miraculous as it seems in each case, for millenia.

Someone has to produce the next generation's liberated children, some say. I think this is self-delusion. There's many a surprise between the way a mother tries to raise her child and the adult who develops from the interaction of mother, home, heredity, individual temperament, environment, chance and whatever else it is that makes us different from and similar to each other. Women who believe the influence of a mother is primary need to reflect upon the variety of personality and politics among their own sisters and brothers and that to be found among their most "liberated" friends. Are our siblings like us? Are we like our mothers? If we are loving, independent, talented Lesbians, and/or want our daughters to be the same, will we raise them like our mothers raised us? AHA! See the problem?

When a woman tells me she wants to have a baby because she "loves children," I feel pity for the child she may have. Her statement reveals her belief in the stereotypes of young human beings that are not likely to be found in individual young persons, including her own. "Loving" children in the abstract, as an identifiable group, is not unlike "loving" Jews or Asians or Gaymen for their positive stereotypes. Child-free women, frequently, do not realize that babies are persons, just like anybody else. They come equipped with their own temperaments and aptitudes which develop into individual personalities while they are still babies. What if the baby develops a personality which doesn't appeal to us? What if the child grows into a toddler we don't particularly like? What if s/he turns out too active or too tidy or too serious or too silly or too loud or too smart or too dumb or too quick or too slow or too uncoordinated or too boring or. . .goddess forgive us. . .too homely. . . for our taste? I am speaking heresy, I know; but I am also speaking truth, a truth that mothers seldom admit. Just as our mothers were "stuck" with us (Did that please them? Do they ever wish they had some other woman for their daughter?), so we are "stuck" with our children.

Some Lesbians are choosing to have babies because they want to love and be loved by someone forever, NO MATTER WHAT! This, too, is a delusion. As a love relationship, motherhood bears some resemblance to that of an arranged marriage, wherein a woman chooses, or is forced, to enter a relationship with a person she does not know, but whom she is expected to love and take care of until one of them dies. No one, not even a mother, can promise to feel love always. We can feel and act upon what seems to be unbreakable ties of loyalty and duty to the members of one's blood family, including one's mother or one's child; but that does not mean that we love them. Some of us can even admit to no longer loving a sibling or a parent. Mothers, however, are not likely to confess a lack of love for their child because not to love or no longer to love one's child is supposed to be the ultimate mother sin, worse than any kind of child abuse done in the name of love, and *EVERY MOTHER KNOWS THIS*. But when love is the exchange, there are no guarantees; and this is true in spite of vows at a Lesbian commitment ceremony or the co-mingled blood and tears of this most intimate and intense physical act, childbirth.

The belief that mothers love their children unconditionally, unselfishly, undyingly is a myth, a myth that keeps women trying, trying, trying to "do the right thing" for our children, to please, to understand, to forgive, to rescue them, over and over and over again, no matter what our real feelings might be, if we can even sort them out. Unconditional mother love is the companion of the myth that women ". . .can't help loving that man of mine."

This reminds me of boy children. Elizabeth Cady Stanton, the influential nineteenth century feminist and the mother of seven children, wrote this: "It is folly to talk of a mother molding the character of her son, when all mankind, backed up by law and public sentiment, conspire to destroy her influence." I can swear to the truth of that. It is too painful to describe what it is like to watch the growing to manhood of a much loved boy child, and to experience his exercise of that manhood in its maturity. Our daughters, at least, are sister sufferers under patriarchy, and their behavior, even when we abhor it, is behavior we understand.

To believe that one's child will love her mother forever is a particularly cruel self-deception. The library is filled with books which flaunt the most virulent mother hatred, and the culture is rife with anti-mother jokes. A visit to the neighborhood nursing home or the sight of a bag lady in a doorway should convince anyone that birthing a child is no guarantee there will be someone to take loving care of us in our old age.

The desire to have a child in order to insure some immortality, so there will be something to show you were here, alive on this earth, after you leave it, is a very powerful, atavistic feeling. I don't know if it is enough, however, to fuel a mother's spirits, even for as short a period as the childbirth experience.

I do believe that many Lesbians having babies now are doing so in response to that all-pervasive, hard to resist, ages old, patriarchal teaching that having a baby is the most fulfilling, most rewarding, most important activity a woman can undertake. . .and that there is something wrong with those women who don't believe this. . . or who don't have children if they can. This is untrue. When we remember all the women whose work fulfilled them, whose work made a difference to others, women who live on in their work, it is no coincidence that most of them were not mothers of children. That some mothers also were achieving women only reminds us of their scarcity in a world full of mothers.

Men love to quote Francis Bacon who wrote, "Men who have children give hostages to fortune," though Bacon's child bride managed the kids and the house while he became famous for his fulfilling, creative, non-reproductive work. No, in a world organized for men, it is the children of *women* who are hostages to fortune. It is women whose child-bearing and child-rearing are the beloved obstacles to study, concentration, time, opportunity, and all the rest that goes into nurturing a talent to maturity.

Of course, most people, even most Lesbians, are not gifted with great talent that needs nurturing; and most of us are never going to make some enormous difference in the world. And, given the economic oppression of women, we are more likely to have boring, dead-end jobs than exciting, challenging ones. This makes the prospect of becoming a mother very appealing. In the first place, even though it isn't revolutionary in the cosmic sense, having a baby is certainly miraculously creative to the woman having one. And who is more important to a child than her mother? We've all had mothers, and we may love her, hate her, respect, despise or pity her; but all of us know her importance in our lives. And that is why so many women, Lesbians included, have babies. Being a mother makes a woman feel important.

But choosing motherhood is so. . .so. . .so final. When people talk about making a career change, they do not mean giving up motherhood! Motherhood is forever.

Women considering motherhood need to know that whenever something bad happens to one's child, from the sniffles to death by drowning, almost everyone will judge it to be somehow your fault, and *YOU WILL AGREE* with the judgment. You will be blamed for birth defects, emotional disturbances, learning disabilities, colic, every accident no matter where it happens or who was caretaking at the time, poor performance on tests and on the ball field, talking in school and not talking in school, "early" sexual development, anorexia, alcohol and drug-abuse. You will love and/or protect the child "too much" or "too little." And for a Lesbian mother, the problem is bound to be worse. Whatever isn't blamed on her "faulty" mothering can be attributed to her sexual "deviance."

Which brings me to the "joys" of motherhood. When I started analyzing them, I realized that the joys I experienced were at least two-thirds the feeling of a most intense sense of relief, relief that flooded my body, filled my heart, eased my mind and soothed my spirit. The first time this happened was right after the birth of my first child, when I awoke from an anesthesia-induced sleep to hear my mother say, "You had a boy and he is perfectly healthy." The feeling came with the "perfectly healthy" part of the statement.

This feeling of relief, which passes for joy, came regularly after its first appearance, more or less intensely depending upon the event that triggered it. When a child did not have the suspected leukemia; when, countless times, they were only late coming home, not. . .; when a suspected fractured skull was only a concussion; when "she was run over" meant by a bike, not a car; when she was not pregnant, when she was not pregnant, when she was not pregnant; when. . . . Of course there are the lesser reliefs when a mother learns the child didn't lie, steal, hit, sneak, or admits a misdeed and is sorry; and the countless times when, whatever the news is, it isn't as awful as what was expected. And this process is never-ending. I don't have the every hour-every day happenings to trigger the joys of relief now that my children are adults; but they come often enough to keep me going. And now I have five grandchildren and one more on the way! Only my death will release me from these kinds of "joys" and from the worry, terror, anguish, and heartache which precedes them.

I will not describe any of the times when the worry, terror and anguish and heartache were followed by more of the same. I can only say that no other relationship, not even the one with one's own mother, can equal motherhood for opportunities to experience all of the above.

So having said all this, do I think Lesbians should not have babies. No, I don't think that either. I cannot think of any "good" reasons for having babies, and can think of many for passing up this "womanly" activity. Still, I must be honest and tell all the truth of it. I say that in my next life I want to be a sterile female so that I can experience the joys of a child-free life. I say "sterile" female because I am afraid that, given the opportunity, I might just do it again. Why? Well, I am crazy about my kids, even now, even though I hated being their mother many times and for long periods of time. I love them more or less depending. . . . I respect them more or less depending. . . . Some of my most satisfying life experiences were mother-experiences. However, *ALL* of my worst life experiences originated with my children, too. Motherhood can be a joyful, interesting and satisfying relationship; but it is also terrible, terrible. If I had had the freedom to choose, knowing then what I know now, would I have chosen mother-hood? I can't be sure, but I don't think so. It is still too soon for me to know if the satisfactions of being a mother will outweigh the anguish, will make the mothering worth the trouble and pain -- and I have been mothering for thirty-five years. That's something to think about, isn't it?

HETEROSEXUAL SPILLOVER *April, 1988*

A Lesbian couple I know celebrated their second anniversary recently. They have a strong sexual attraction for each other, and both have a sharp, quick, witty sense of humor. The early months of their relationship were filled with sex and laughter. "I've never had so much fun," they would say. "I've never had such good sex." They met each other's friends, but they were alone together most of the time. There were not enough hours in the day, what with work and necessary maintenance chores separating them. Everything superfluous was abandoned in their desire to be in each other's presence. Even when apart, they managed to speak on the phone several times daily. To increase their shared time, they began doing chores together, laundry at first, then grocery shopping and errands. Still, it wasn't enough. Finally, inexorably, they came to the inevitable discovery that they were meant for each other, fated to be together for life, to live together happily ever after.

So they moved in together and almost immediately began to see a Lesbian therapist to help them work out their differences. Differences! What had they in common besides their sexual attraction and sense of humor? They were both women, white, Lesbian, American; but they had been born and raised in different generations, classes, religions. Their differences encompass attitudes, values, behaviors, as well as personality and style and individual preferences. One is used to doing for herself, and doing without. One wants a baby. One loves her work and brings it home with her. One worries. One hates dogs. One eats lunch out. One is athletic. One seldom does housework or cooks. One sews. One prefers PBS and classical music. One spends money. One does not. They do not like each other's friends. "We would never have lasted two years if it hadn't been for our therapist," they tell me. "We are learning to work with our differences, to change, to compromise," they say.

I am a cynic. I can't see inside their relationship. I see only the outside, and I am not impressed. Their compromises look like losses to me. They do not invite friends to their house. Neither plays softball. They seldom watch television and frequently eat out. The worrier tries to keep things to herself. The one who does housework is trying to relax in a messy house. They do not have a bank account. They have a dog. The one who wants a baby still wants a baby. And it looks like they have developed a new problem which intensifies the differences they brought with them into the relationship -- resentment!

So why do they stay together? They say they love each other. I suggest they are more likely to learn to work lovingly with each other's differences if they live separately. They are insulted. I'm thinking of practical things. Separate homes to clean, or not clean, to have, or not have, babies and dogs in, separate bank accounts and separate bills to pay, would erase many problems their differences cause. They won't consider it, think I do not take their relationship seriously. Besides, they can afford a nicer place together than they can apart. But the real, the important reason they live together and will continue to live together is because they have a serious, committed relationship and are each other's family. While they are unconventional enough to be Lesbians, they are not unconventional enough to develop living arrangements different from the heterosexual nuclear family model. Their relationship is suffering from what I call "heterosexual spillover into Lesbian life," and in this instance, I believe the spillover will be fatal.

Heterosexual spillover into Lesbian lives occurs when we try to apply those societal values, attitudes and beliefs that are necessary for the preservation of heterosexuality, as it is lived in our culture, to Lesbianism. The most blatant example of heterosexual spillover is wife/husband role playing by Lesbian couples, but there are a myriad of more subtle ways in which that spillover infects our Lesbian lives. Believing that

Lesbian couples, like their heterosexually married counterparts, should share everything, including housing, is another.

It is not unusual for Lesbian couples to dissolve their love relationships every few years for any number of reasons. When this happens, we say, "It just didn't work out." Whether or not we are glad that the particular relationship is over, we usually feel a sense of failure and a concern that there is something intrinsically wrong with us because we can't/won't/don't want to have "long-term" relationships. We think we may not be serious enough, mature enough, trusting enough for a long-term commitment, that we are "afraid of intimacy." All that may or may not be true about our characters, but what we are doing is negatively comparing our short-term relationships to heterosexual marriage as if the long-term heterosexual marriage was an ideal to strive for.

The heterosexual marriage/nuclear family is the model for correct, ethical, moral, state supported and sanctioned sexual relationships in our country. To be "successful" as a woman, all of us are supposed to be married, ideally only once, monogamously, with children, for many years till death -- his or ours. Anything else is failure -- ours, not his. This ideal of womanly success has been pounded into us from our earliest days, surrounds us in just about everything we experience every day of our lives. It is not surprising that we bring so much of it into our Lesbian lives. It requires constant vigilance to keep heterosexual spillover from infecting us.

The truth is that we have no idea how women (or men) might behave in their love, sexual, reproductive, companion relationships when we are free of personal and institutional male supremacy. All we really "know" is how all kinds of relationships exist in a patriarchy. I think that it is likely that all women will behave much the way Lesbians do now *when they are free to do so.* Some women will meet a person with whom they are so completely compatible that they mate for life. There would be no enforceable promise of "till death us do part" of course. It will be common knowledge that no one can be sure such initial compatibility will continue until it does, and enforced feigned compatibility will be seen as an horrific perversion of human relations. Some women will be lovers with many different persons, serially and/or concurrently. Women who choose to have babies will not confuse reproduction with sex. Women may live with one person in an intimately compatible, sexual or non-sexual relationship while enjoying intimate sexual and/or non-sexual relationships with many or few others. We may live alone or in community with others for short or long periods of time. How can we know! We have no idea the extent of women's capacity to love. Even our guesses, our wishes are tainted by sexism.

In the meantime, I wish Lesbians would affirm how revolutionary our relationships are, how revolutionary are relationships based on women's happiness. I wish we could appreciate our courage when we take the emotional risks inherent in beginning new relationships and in experimenting in different ways of being together. I wish we would stop negatively comparing our "short-term" relationships to the length of time women and men live together in "holy matrimony," and favorably comparing our "long-term" relationships to that institution. Ideally, Lesbians stay together as long as it pleases us and in whatever arrangement pleases us. Let's not permit heterosexual spillover to distort the reality of our personal freedom to create relationships that serve the needs and desires of women in all our interesting diversity.

By the way, I started this piece last spring and since then my friends' relationship broke up. It is one of those nasty break-ups filled with recriminations, back-biting, accusations. I hate it. I know they could have laughed and loved with each other for as long as it pleased them, and then moved on when or if their life situations and needs changed *without* feeling betrayed if only... Oh well, perhaps next time!

BREAKING UP IS HARD TO DO
November, 1983

Even if the Lesbian Nation existed, breaking-up would still be THE terrible part of being a Lesbian. Perhaps this adult rejection of, or our rejection by, another woman echoes in our irrational core, the infant-mother feeling state. Perhaps a superior capacity for emotional bonding and intensity, which makes our relationships so spirit-satisfying, brings with it that sublime torture known as breaking-up (or its euphemism, "redefining our relationship"). Whatever its cause, the pain of breaking-up a Lesbian sexual love relationship can be so severe that some Lesbians stay together for years rather than endure it, while some others take up with men rather than risk a repetition.

I have suffered only one Lesbian break-up so far, but it was one of the most painful, difficult, shattering experiences of the forty-five years, six months and eight days of my life which preceded it. My family and friends were shocked by the depth of my grieving; and I was stunned by it myself. I promised myself to never risk even the possibility of a recurrence. I gave not one second's thought to the "take up with men" solution, but decided I would not allow myself to get involved in another sexual love relationship with a woman. I imagined my future self, serenely aloof, nun-like, the loving friend of many women, but no woman's lover. Before I had replaced my waterbed with the austere, narrow bedstead of the celibate nun, however, I became so intensely involved in a sexual love relationship with a close, good friend that the chance for aloof serenity was gone!

Since that time, I've learned that my behavior was typically Lesbian. We are positive that this is the VERY LAST TIME we will suffer this way, until we find ourselves involved with another irresistible woman. Ah! This is one of the joys of being a Lesbian - the experience of the irresistibleness of woman being herself with her peers.

I always tell Lesbians with broken hearts who think they will never find another woman with just that perfect combination of qualities as the one for whom they are grieving, to make a list of all the women they would have a brief affair with if the other woman suggested it. "Oh, there is no woman I am even the least bit attracted to," is the response I usually get. "What if Gloria Steinem called? Barbara Jordan? Martina Navritilova? Audre Lorde? Alix Dobkin?" Once the list is a possibility and then a reality, any red-blooded Lesbian can soon begin to add names a little closer to home. This is a pleasant way to bring a little hope to a broken heart.

I believe many break-ups last months longer than is good for both women, dragging on the sorrow of disengagement, forever it seems. The relationship is at the should-we-try-to-continue-the-relationship stage. Both women cry and talk with friends separately. They have interminable conversations with each other on the subject in bed, on the phone at work, driving to meetings and social events. They may be seeing a Lesbian therapist for relationship counseling. The women are trying to do the right thing in their womanly way and this takes time.

There comes a time in this process, sometimes, when one of the women realizes, with absolute certainty, that the lover relationship between them is over. This knowing may break her heart, or it may not. Whatever she feels about the relationship's end, she decides to keep her certainty to herself instead of acting upon it by telling her lover and getting on to the next step -- dividing the books, for example. Perhaps she can't bear the next step or she thinks her lover can't bear it, or they promised to wait an arbitrary length of time before "doing anything."

This inaction prolongs the process of breaking-up at the point where it is likely to cause the most damage to the respect, friendship and love between them. This is the time of accusation, justification and, if we are not careful, vilification. The possibility for friendship between former lovers frequently perishes from the rancor produced by the emotional exhaustion of an over-long break-up. I think we need to say, *out loud*, our certainty of a relationship's end when we experience it. Our womanly desire to avoid hurting someone is misplaced here.

Sometimes, though, the motive for silence is less than pure. Sometimes the one who knows the relationship is over feels guilty because she no longer wants to continue in a lover relationship with the woman who loves her. She goes through the motions of working it out in the hope that her lover will decide she wants out, too, or, at least, will become pleasantly reconciled to the break-up, so that she doesn't have to feel guilty for hurting this woman she loved and so on, and so on.

Sometimes the motive for prolonging the process is vindictiveness. In this instance, the woman who knows the relationship is over does not want the break-up. She considers herself an "injured party." Acting as if there is still hope for the continuation of the relationship, she can punish her lover who is desperately trying to do the right thing and is feeling terrible about whatever she did or did not do to jeopardize the relationship.

A recurring break-up problem among Lesbians is the "we want to remain good friends" one. This is a particularly thorny one when it occurs in the break-up of a couple in which one woman is leaving or has left the other for love of a third. Here we have one woman feeling guilty and responsible for inflicting pain upon a woman she loves, but no longer wants a lover relationship with. She is also impatient and resentful of the time and energy she uses in helping her former lover adjust when it keeps her from her new lover. The former lover, on the other hand, is suffering the worst of breaking-up feelings, those of rejection and diminished self-esteem. She also feels angry, foolish, and jealous. Yet these two women are trying to feel and behave with each other as good friends do. Impossible!

For example, a good friend of the woman who left might say, "I heard you are madly in love. How wonderful for you. When can you and she come to dinner so I can meet her?" Would a newly rejected, good friend-lover be able to say this and mean it? This is tantamount to expecting her to say that she is happy her lover is happy with someone else, while she herself is very unhappy because her lover is no longer with her.

Or the good friend of the rejected lover might call to see how her friend is doing. Is she sleeping better? Is she crying less? Would she like company for dinner? For the woman who precipitated her emotional crisis to phone, asking if she is handling herself well, is patronizing. "I've broken your heart; how well are you taking it? Can you have dinner with me without crying and making a spectacle of yourself?"

Certainly, I think we all should make every attempt to see that our break-ups are lovingly accomplished, no easy task, but one that can occur with the help of our friends. I feel very strongly, however, that breaking-up Lesbian lovers need to give themselves as much time as it takes to become "former lovers" before they try to act like "good friends." There is great pressure on Lesbians breaking-up, from friends and from themselves, to do the politically correct thing -- and make all their friends more comfortable -- by acting as if everything is fine when it is not. I've seen women do emotional damage to themselves by trying to force a friendship before they are ready because it is the Lesbian thing to do. I think a lover relationship which is based upon solid liking and respect can develop into a friendship, and taking the space of a few months, with little or no contact to heal the wounds won't impede it.

It has been my experience, by the way, that the aggressive insistence upon being "good friends" at once, frequently comes from the woman who leaves because she wants her ex-lover to act as if she is no longer hurting so she can enjoy her new relationship without feeling bad about the ex -- or from the woman who is left because she can keep her former lover around to punish, with her sighs and long face, this woman who has the nerve to be happy when she is not!

In my opinion, the most important thing to remember during breaking-up -- though we do not want others to remind us -- is that this period of misery will eventually end; and we will be happy again - even though we are sure we will not. It is helpful, too, to remember the respect we have for the lover, even when we are too upset to feel it or when she is behaving so terribly. This will keep us from saying things about her that we would regret later -- when we are good friends again who once were lovers.

LOVE, YOUR MAGIC SPELL
IS EVERYWHERE *April, 1983*

> *Just because it's over*
> *Doesn't mean it wasn't love*
> > --Edna St. Vincent Millay

When I was a feminist living a heterosexual life and met my first out Lesbians, I thought they were sort of unstable. I soon learned they frequently developed long-term friendship relationships with their former lovers. I saw they had long-term friendship relationships with other women as well. I knew them as dependable workers at their jobs and in the Women's Liberation Movement. I even knew them to be caring perfectionists in their mothering. Yet I continued to believe that Lesbians were less stable than I was because their loving/sexual relationships didn't last for years and years. It didn't take me long to realize I was seeing Lesbians only in their sexual lives, a typical non-Lesbian, homophobic attitude. So I cleaned that up and decided that Lesbians were dependable and stable in all aspects of their lives EXCEPT in their sexual relationships.

Then one day, thank Sappho, I realized I was being stupid again. I was comparing women who lived free, consensual sexual lives with their equals to women whose loving (or not so loving) sexual relationships are rooted in religious, cultural, economic, familial, legal and frequently physical coercion and/or violence -- and judged the free women unstable and the unfree women (myself included) stable. It was as if I was comparing pre-Civil War free Black Americans to those in slavery, and deciding that the slaves were more stable because they "kept" the same "job" for their entire lives! It was as if I compared people who move often with the Birdman of Alcatraz! "Aha," I thought, "is it possible that women who live heterosexual lives might have sexual relationship histories similar to those of Lesbians if they were as free as Lesbians to do so?" I mentally reviewed my own heterosexual history and decided that, in fact, it is heterosexist female slavery which keeps most women in those long-term heterosexual relationships called marriage to which the relationships of free Lesbians are unfavorably compared. This insight gave birth to many of my most cherished theories about Lesbians as well as moving me further along the Lesbian path.

For example, I realized that Lesbians tend to be very romantic. We believe in love with a fervor which surpasses that of the Pope for Catholicism. Lesbians believe in romantic love, not only at seventeen, but at seventy. We believe in it in all its manifestations: infatuation, love-at-first-sight, getting-to-know-each-other-first-love, brief erotic experiences, life-long monogamous love commitment, life-long non-monogamous love commitment, serial monogamy love commitments, brief love affairs, *menage-a-trois* (women only, of course), communal living with the entire household as loving sexual partners, and non-sexual committed long-term love partnerships. (I've been told that some Lesbians also believe in long-term unrequited love too, though I've never met any.)

Because Lesbians, in their personal lives, exist outside the patriarchal state, free from male power and control, they can be as free as their individual psyches allow them to be, to act on these beliefs about love. Lesbians are free to live out whatever variety of Lesbian relationships fit who they are at any given time. Societal condemnation of female "promiscuity" and pre- and extramarital sexual activity does not inhibit Lesbians, who are sexual outlaws already, to the extent it controls the behavior of other women. Also, as Lesbians we need not fear losing our "reputation," or being the kind of girl no man would marry! In addition, we are much freer to enjoy casual erotic experiences with women we do not know well since woman/woman violence, while it does exist, is miniscule compared to the violence endemic in woman/man casual encounters. And we won't get pregnant, or "have to get married" as a result. Our outlaw status, therefore, allows us to act on those lovely, lusty, romantic feelings far more often and with more satisfactory results, than our sisters living heterosexual lives.

Certainly, women who relate to men believe in romantic love too, and would like to act on those feelings. However, the belief that they are destined for marriage and motherhood is inhibiting. Also, their experiences dating men teach them to be very careful. They have to consider all those problems mentioned above before they act, and then they most often have to say "no" to the experience. Too many Mr. Goodbars and unwanted pregnancies await them. Besides, most women living heterosexual lives are firmly committed to the Prince Charming variety of romantic love: girl meets boy, girl marries boy, girl lives happily ever after. This variety of romantic love is almost always doomed to failure because marriage transforms Prince Charming into King of the Castle, in other words, Head of the Household. The romantic woman becomes a wife, and marriage becomes her occupation as well as her loving sexual relationship. She picks up and puts away his underwear and socks; he does not do the same for her. It is practically impossible for her to sustain her romantic feelings for the person who relates to her as his mother, a "privileged domestic," the mother of his children, and his sexual property. She learns to settle for the vicarious romance of her fantasy life, books and films, and the goings on of the famous, after her romantic attempts -- candlelight dinners, love notes in his briefcase or lunch box, gifts on no special occasion -- are ridiculed or else treated as one more wifely duty. Yes, that's right. Keeping the romance alive in a woman/man relationship (marriage or not) is the duty of the woman. Lesbians send balloons to their lovers because they feel like it and think it romantic. Women living heterosexual lives can never know FOR SURE if any of their romantic impulses are authentic or if they are simply the acting out of learned behavior called "pleasing your man," or "keeping your man."

The fact is that heterosexual relationships are not intended to please women; they are designed to serve men and to sustain patriarchal control over women's lives, including our sexual and reproductive capacities. All women are taught from infancy to expect happiness (in this life, or in the next) from serving "our man." Remember Adam's helpmate, Eve! We are taught there is something "wrong" with women who do not base their happiness on that service, and with women who do not find happiness in that service. Lesbians live in direct contradiction to this basic societal belief about how women achieve happiness. No wonder others think us unhappy and unstable! We believe in being happy in love, not in service. We willingly sacrifice social approval, joint tax returns, "family" insurance policies and the like for the personal freedom inherent in

Lesbian life. This personal freedom to love whom and how we choose is the basis of Lesbianism.

Thus, it is illogical for non-Lesbians and Lesbians alike to expect Lesbians to express their love and sexuality the way women who relate to men express theirs. To allow the lack of freedom forced upon women in heterosexual relationships to be the model for Lesbians is illogical. To think something is wrong with Lesbians who cannot, or who choose not, to live within relationships which no longer please them, as non-Lesbian women are expected to, is illogical as well. A friend expressed a Lesbian truth well when she said, "I was happier in the year and a half of my first Lesbian relationship than my mother has been in forty-two years of marriage." Socrates was correct when he noted: "True love can only exist between equals," and the poet knew whereof she spoke: "Just because it's over, doesn't mean it wasn't love."

[7]At the time of legal Black slavery in the USA, individual slaveowners made rules governing the lives of their human property, including those for marriage. Many slaveowners, who thought themselves "good Christians," did not want to be responsible for "putting asunder" a Christian couple. The solution they devised was NOT to discontinue the sale of slave couples to separate and distant plantations. Instead, they denied slaves a lawful (i.e. Christian) wedding and instituted their own ceremony for slaves during which the lucky couple who had received permission to marry from their owner was expected to "legalize" the relationship by jumping over a broomstick. Only heterosexual couples received permission to jump over the broomstick, of course.

VI. Happy Beginnings

REPARATIONS *June, 1989*

We met a woman recently who had "forgotten" she was sexually molested by her father's brother throughout her childhood and early adolescence. She lived her life as best she could while suffering periodic bouts of severe, frequently suicidal, depression for which she could find no reason. She was in therapy for about seventeen years before she remembered. She confronted her uncle, told her parents, her siblings, his neighbors, everyone she could. Her uncle admitted his crimes against her, swore he had not touched another child. The family was in an uproar. "Did he touch you?" "Did he touch him?" "Did he touch her?" It was confirmed. Only her. Now they knew why she had been so troubled for so long. The family rallied round her. "What shall we do?" They offered to banish him from their large, close, exuberant family. She decided she did not want that, though she was pleased they all were willing to do it. They had a gathering to discuss what to do about Uncle Joe. He could not be forgiven without some kind of reparations. They had Mary tote up all the money it cost for seventeen years of therapy, the days of work lost, the medical bills. They, not Mary, presented him with the bill. With Mary's assent, he

224

just deeded over to her a lot on the St.Johns River in St. Augustine, Florida, valued at forty-five thousand dollars, as a beginning. Now *there's* a model family!

BRIEF AFFAIR   *February, 1990*

Marilyn and Irene met in the Spring of 1977 when Marilyn was working for the Gay and Lesbian Community Services Center. Irene came to a Center fund-raiser to hear Kate Millett read from her work-in-progress, *Sita*. During intermission, Marilyn handed out flyers announcing her new Center project, a Tuesday night rap group for Lesbians over forty. The building was packed, and she enjoyed herself as she threaded her way among the women, watching for signs of aging on their faces. She spotted a likely candidate for the group leaning against a post, out of reach. "Yoo Hoo," she called, waving the flyer at the woman. "Here's something for you." There was no response. She gave a flyer to a nearby woman to pass on while she continued her attempts to catch the eye of her quarry. The flyer arrived at its destination and a puzzled Irene looked at it, looked at Marilyn, and then looked around for an "older" woman to pass it on to. Marilyn laughed. "No! No! No! It's for you." Irene was incredulous. "Me?" "Yes," was the response. "You with the gray hair. I know you're over forty. Come to the rap group and we'll talk about it." Irene smiled. Marilyn smiled. A thin zzzzzzzzzzzzzzzt of sex attraction warmed them. Then Irene turned to speak to her lover and Marilyn turned to give a flyer to someone else.

That might have been the end of it, except that Irene was feeling a little tied down, squeezed in, by Tina, with whom she was trying to have a new kind of relationship, a non-monogamous, sexual friendship kind of relationship. More as a gesture of independence than anything else, Irene decided to check out the rap group, one event where Tina, who was thirty-two, was not likely to appear. What a stir she created during those spring and summer evenings at the Center! Most of the participants of the Over Forty rap were Lesbians who had recently lost their lovers to death or another woman. They were "old fashioned," Old Gay Lesbians, looking for new lovers, not new ideas or new ways to be Lesbians. Irene was fifty years old, one of them, but only in her history. She was afire with new ideas: holistic healing, the hippie movement, humanism and Lesbian feminism. She was experimenting, had one lover, two lovers, three lovers, a *menage-a-trois*, all of which she discussed in the group.

Marilyn was afire herself, though from a somewhat different source. At forty-five years old, she was a year and a half into her first Lesbian relationship and was utterly infatuated with Leslie and all things Lesbian. In Irene she found someone with a fervor for Lesbian talk that matched her own. They talked at group, and they talked over coffee after group. They acknowledged the sexual buzz that accompanied conversations, but admitted they were not interested in being "more than friends," at least not then. Should either of them change her mind, the other would be the first to know. In the meantime they would continue their friendship, expand it to include Tina and Leslie, and see each other without their lovers *only* at the rap group. No point in asking for trouble!

So Marilyn and Leslie had Irene and Tina to dinner at Leslie's. Then Irene and Tina had Marilyn and Leslie for swimming and barbecue at Irene's. During the months that followed, the couples invited each other to meals, parties, events. They met each other's friends. Irene and Leslie admired each other, two dykes from the old days who had "made it, a house in the suburbs, a swimming pool and a sports car!" as Leslie used to say. Even so, Irene found Leslie "difficult" and Marilyn found Tina "impossible." Because their friendship was precious to them, the two colluded in making the foursome "work." They became almost as attentive to the moods and idiosyncrasies of the other's lover as they were to their own. They were especially careful to include Leslie and Tina in their endless conversations that occurred when they were together.

Irene and Marilyn also talked on the phone. Often! When they were *alone!* They talked for hours about politics, food, travel, books, family, friends. . .lovers. Irene "explained" Leslie's Old Gay attitudes to Marilyn, who was frequently upset, angry, in tears as she muddled through her Lesbian initiation. They discussed the differences between Lifelong Lesbians, like Irene and Leslie, and "Women's Liberation Movement," Lesbians-Come-Lately like Marilyn. They dissected that topic so often and in such detail that they were able to conduct workshops at Lesbian conferences that summer and fall titled, "Old Gay and New: A Dialogue."

By November Marilyn was experiencing her first broken heart and the beginning of her first Lesbian breakup. She was one of ten "out" Lesbians chosen to represent California at the International Women's Year Conference in Houston, Texas, and Leslie didn't want to go with her. "She's seeing someone else," Irene insisted. "She wouldn't lie," cried the new Lesbian. "She would," replied the voice of experience.

Irene was having her own troubles with Tina. Her new way of being a Lesbian, open, free, non-monogamous was not working out the way she hoped. Tina was at least as possessive and jealous and troublesome as any of her Old Gay lovers. Irene wanted to attend the Houston Conference with Marilyn, but didn't dare. She knew Tina was capable of following her and creating a scene.

Marilyn and Leslie broke-up on New Year's Day. Marilyn's first Lesbian romance was over. "First and last," she declared to Irene, who had stopped by to see how she was doing. "I will never go through this again. A broken heart is too painful, too humiliating." Irene knew better. "I swear to you, Marilyn, there is a wonderful woman out there, just waiting for you." Marilyn was not impressed. She was not going to risk it.

"I don't need a lover. I don't need anymore drama. I may have brief affairs, but nothing more. I'm going to live my life surrounded by my women friends, the way I did before I became a Lesbian." Irene gave her a consoling, friendly pat and went home where Tina was fomenting drama.

By late January, Marilyn was ready for a brief affair. First she called Irene. "I am ready to change the nature of our relationship anytime you are," she stated, causing Irene to lapse into speechlessness. When Irene recovered, she stammered something about having to "think about it." Marilyn assured her that she was not expecting anything. She was simply activating her list of women she would like to have a brief affair with. "I called you first because I don't know how to get hold of Alix Dobkin, Audre Lorde or Agnes Moorehead!" They both laughed. The friendship remained intact.

The phone calls continued. Marilyn soon realized that the tenor of the conversation had changed for her, that she was waiting for Irene to take her up on her offer. She began to feel awkward. She decided to give the possibility of a brief affair with Irene one more try, before dismissing it for good. She called her. "Sandakan Eight" is playing at the Los Feliz on Thursday, Friday and Saturday nights this week. I'd like to see it with you. Are you interested?" There followed a long, long pause. "Yes," was the answer. "How about Friday?" Marilyn could hear Irene's smile. She asked, "Your car or mine?" "Mine," Irene replied, and the die was cast.

Irene kissed Marilyn on the mouth before they went into the theater, letting her know that she knew what was going on. As a result, they don't remember the movie well. They were unusually quiet on the drive back. "Would you like to come in for coffee, Irene?" "Of course." "You do know it's my bed I'm inviting you into," Marilyn continued. Again Irene responded, "Of course." And into bed they went.

Several mornings later, after their third night of good sex and sound sleep, Irene and Marilyn were in Marilyn's bedroom drinking coffee and talking. Irene's face turned serious. "I need to warn you not to expect a long relationship with me. I usually last two years before I start getting bored." Marilyn tried not to giggle. "Why are you telling me this? I know your history by now." Then Irene smiled. "Of course," she said. "I've not become lovers with a friend before. I just didn't want you to get the wrong idea." "I haven't," Marilyn assured her. "Have you forgotten? All I want with you is a brief affair." Irene sighed with relief. "A brief affair it is then!"

On Valentine's Day, 1991, neither of them bored yet, Irene and Marilyn commemorated the thirteenth year of their brief affair.

APPENDIX

Since the above essays initially appeared in the Lesbian News from 1982 on, we have included the original publication dates. Some of the titles have changed. We have provided the original titles here in this appendix. Many of Marilyn Murphy's Lesbianic Logic columns were reprinted throughout the years, and we've listed those years as well.

Clothespin Fever Press, Los Angeles, 1991

LOVE, YOUR MAGIC SPELL IS EVERYWHERE, April 1983
MANHATING, part 1 September 1982
MANHATING LESBIAN, originally titled *Manhating II*, October 1982
MANLESSNESS, February 1989
MEMORIES FROM THE GOOD OLD DAYS, September 1989
MOTHER OF THE GROOM, January 1985
NEWFOUNDLAND, originally titled *Notes While Traveling*, December 1986
OLD IS IN, June 1987
    Parts I and II November and December 1982,
THE POWER OF NAMING, February 1991
PRETTY IN PINK. July 1986
PUTTING WOMEN FIRST, originally titled *The Divisive Issue Of Men*, November 1987
REPARATIONS, originally titled *Short Subjects: Summer, '89*, June 1989
SHE'S JEWISH, YOU KNOW! December 1987
THE SUMMER OF '73, July 1985
TERRORISM IN AMERICA, originally titled, *There Is No North*, August 1989
THANKSGIVING DAY, November 1988
THINKING ABOUT BISEXUALITY, February 1984
THINKING ABOUT BOY CHILDREN, originally titled *When Lesbians Put Boys First*, December 1989
WASHINGTON WEEKEND, November 1987
WE ARE FAMILY, August 1983
WOULD KNOWING THIS HAVE MADE A DIFFERENCE? Parts I and II Nov/Dec. 1982, Reprinted March 1988

INDEX